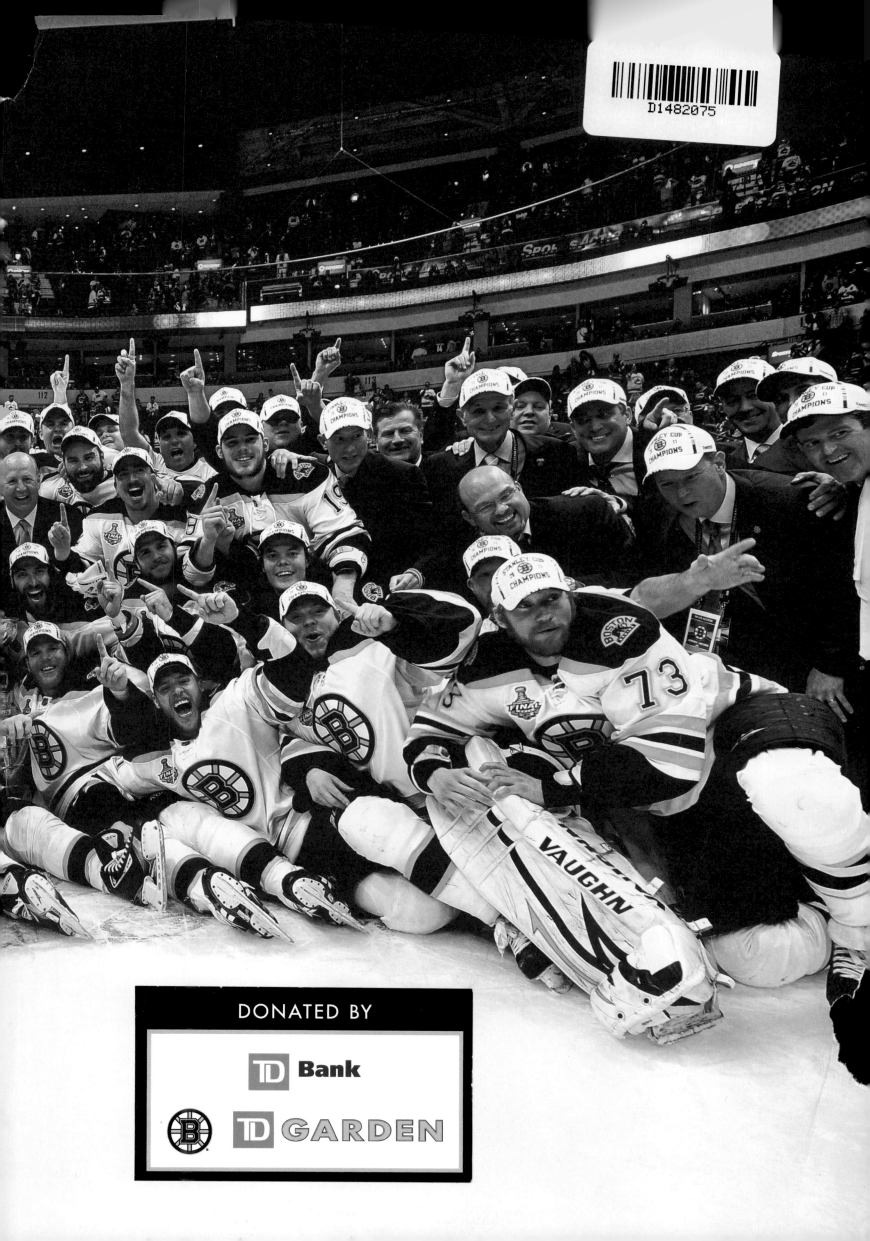

FULL 60+
TO HISTORY

THE INSIDE STORY OF THE 2011 STANLEY CUP CHAMPION BOSTON BRUINS

Foreword by **CAM NEELY**   Introduction by **PETER CHIARELLI**   Afterword by **MARK RECCHI**

Written by **JOHN BISHOP** & **ERIC TOSI**

SKYBOX PRESS • SAN DIEGO, CALIFORNIA

TABLE OF CONTENTS

PURE JOY
JEREMY JACOBS

I remember it as if it were yesterday. We were up 3-0 in Vancouver with about six minutes to go. Security came in and told us it was time to begin to make our way down to the ice. I told them in no uncertain terms that I wasn't going anywhere. Harry Sinden had a rule about goals and minutes left. And it was too early. His rule about jumping the gun on a victory dance—half superstition, half common sense—came from years of playing and being behind the bench. Even if he was off the money this time, a do-or-die contest for all the marbles was far from the right time to test the soundness of this particular Harryism. I was staying put.

So, at the two-minute mark (and not a second before), we began our journey to the ice. As we ran down the stairs, my son Lou said, "They just scored." "Oh, no," I thought, thinking it was Vancouver. But it was us. Caught up in a sweep of bodies, we were propelled forward. The next thing I knew, I was on the ice as the celebration began. It was pure joy. Embracing these young men, whom I began the season with in Prague, and watching them celebrate is something I will never forget. Zee hoisted the Cup and other players followed suit. I was so proud of our players and happy for them. They came together as one of the strongest teams in our history, and each and every player contributed to our success.

During the celebration on the ice I took a moment to sit on the bench. I gave thanks—thanks to the players, Claude and his coaches, Cam, Peter, and the entire support team for sharing this remarkable journey with me and my family; thanks to our fans for sticking with us through the years where we struggled to meet expectations; thanks to the community for embracing us and never forgetting our only goal was to win; and thanks to my wife, Peg, and my family for their unwavering support as we went up hills and down valleys. I was sad that Peg, at home not feeling well, couldn't be with our family enjoying the celebration and capturing the moment, as she always does, with her camera.

Whoever said winning isn't everything has never held the Stanley Cup. There's something magical about that trophy; it is the best trophy in all of sports. So historic. So meaningful. To hold it is to understand what it is to be the best.

The celebration in the locker room with not a dry eye—or shirt, for that matter. Crowds spilling into the streets in Boston. The duck boat parade with more than 1 million fans celebrating their Cup win. All of the journeys the players have made with the Cup this summer with their families, friends, and communities. I know now we've given Boston fans what they so richly deserve: a season to remember and a championship team.

I'm so proud of the men who lace up for each game and everyone who wears the spoked-B in some way. And I'm so pleased to share this official commemorative keepsake. It's been an amazing ride, my friends.

ABOVE: Bruins Owner Jeremy Jacobs, *center*, shared his excitement and pride during the on-ice celebration in Vancouver with his children, *left to right*, Lisann Jacobs, Lou Jacobs, Katie Jacobs Robinson, Lynn Jacobs Reichenbach, Jerry Jacobs Jr. and Charlie Jacobs.

FOREWORD
CAM NEELY

It doesn't seem like that long ago that I was traded to Boston on June 6, 1986—my 21st birthday. I can't believe it's been 25 years.

I remember that it was pre-cell phones; I was working out with some friends, and my younger sister informed me about the trade that would change my life. At the time I was unsure what was in store for me in Boston, but as surprised and anxious as I was to be traded away from my hometown, going to an Original Six franchise was exciting, especially because my style was conducive to what Bruins fans expect from their players.

Boston had always been the kind of team that worked hard and played physical. My approach had always been to do the same, and I was thrilled to find so many like-minded teammates. So many great players had worn the Bruins jersey over the years, and we all loved wearing the Black & Gold.

Our building was small, but I loved playing in the old Garden because the fans were right on top of you, and I embraced the history of this franchise and their fans right away. Likewise, the city embraced all of us players, and as loud as the building got during the regular season, it got that much louder in the playoffs.

We made it to the Stanley Cup Final in 1988 and 1990, but that was as close as I came to winning a championship as a player and as close as our organization had come in several years. I never touched the Stanley Cup, and I was absolutely of that mindset that unless you're part of a team that wins it you just don't touch it.

I can also tell you this: It's much more difficult to lose in the Final than it is in the first round because you know you are just four games away from winning it all. I know that holds true for our fans as well; we were all so close to that sixth Cup.

When I had to retire in 1996, my passion for the Boston Bruins always remained. In 2007, when Charlie Jacobs asked me to get involved in the front office, I was excited but cautious. I wanted to make sure that I was going to enjoy what was asked of me, and I wanted to gauge what the passion level in the organization was for winning the Stanley Cup. Finally, I also needed to be sure that I could have some kind of positive impact on the team. After numerous conversations with Peter Chiarelli, I felt comfortable with my decision to join this group, and I could tell we all shared a common purpose. I was excited to do my part to help build the organization into a winner on and off the ice and bring back the culture of what it means to be a Bruin. It worked out even better than I expected.

In the summer of 2010 I was offered, and was honored to accept, the role of team president. Growing up as a hockey player you never imagine becoming the president of a team. I grew up dreaming of playing in the NHL and competing for the Stanley Cup. As a player, I was always trying to make things happen on the ice and affect the outcome of the games. As the president, I feel the same way. I have the same passion, but it is done in a different way. It certainly was a great thrill and pleasure to be part of the team and the group that returned the Stanley Cup back to Boston.

As the clock was winding down and we knew we were going to be Stanley Cup champions, the thoughts that ran through my head were of my parents, my family, and my many Bruin teammates. I thought about our current players, coaches, and staff and the joy I felt watching them celebrate knowing what they had gone through. I thought about the generations of fans that had stuck by the Bruins while waiting 39 years for the Stanley Cup to come back to Boston and how excited I knew you all would be.

I also thought about how hard we are going to work to do it all over again because of just how great it feels!

As you look forward to our seventh banner, we hope this book rekindles all those feelings over and over. In the interim, we promise to work hard to do the same on the ice each and every season.

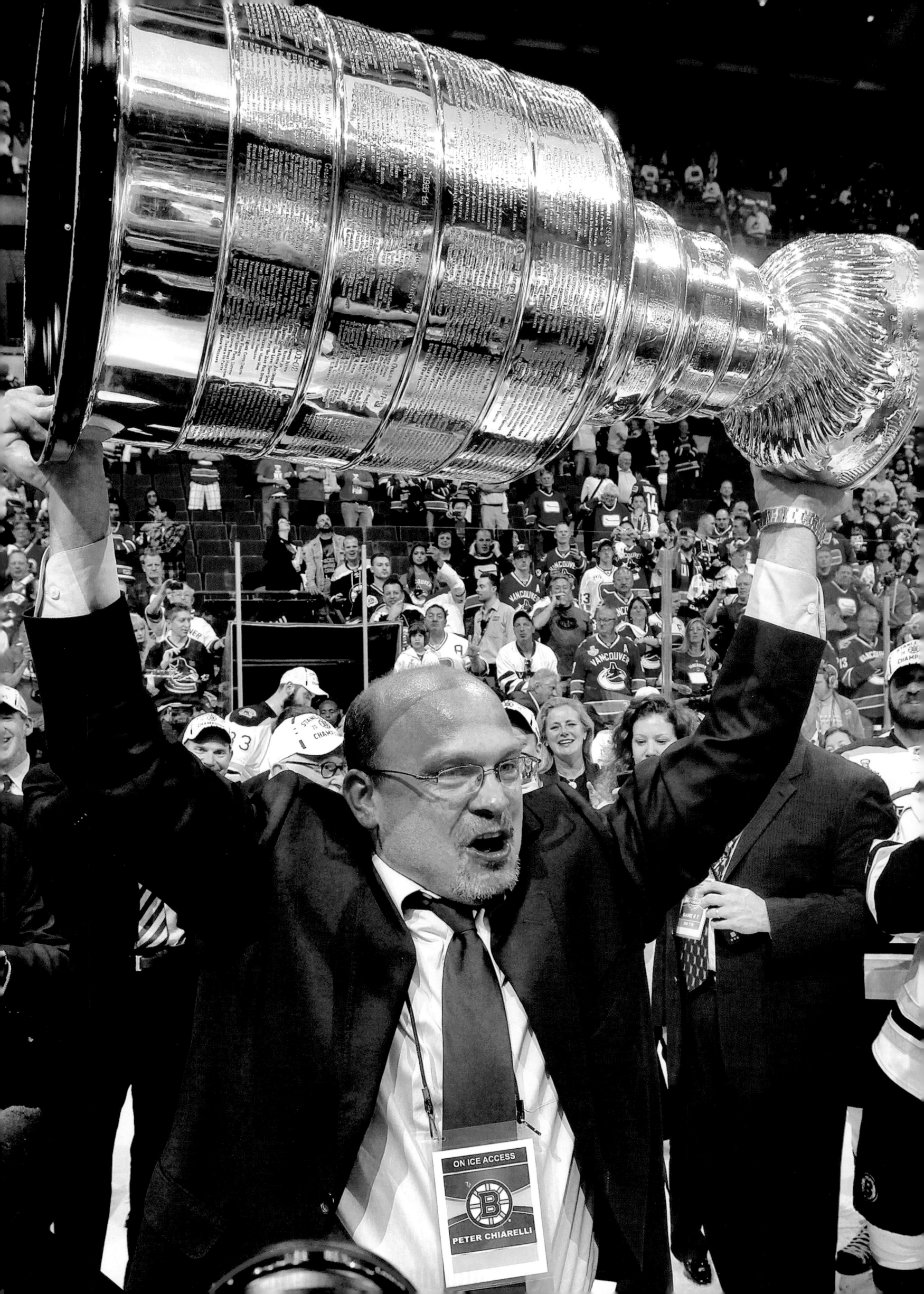

ON ICE ACCESS

PETER CHIARELLI

INTRODUCTION
PETER CHIARELLI

Put simply, this book is the story of our championship season told from the perspective of those who lived it. Through this project, we have essentially opened up our locker room doors in order to bring you inside our team and bring you along for the journey. Insights from our players, coaches, and management will explain why and when we made certain trades, who helped motivate us, and what our themes were throughout the year, including our theme from the playoffs that gave this book its title: *Full 60+ to History*.

While we end this story on top, we actually begin at the bottom.

Heading into the 2010-11 campaign, no one had forgotten the excruciating loss to Philadelphia earlier in the year in the Eastern Conference semifinals, when the Flyers came back from three games down in the series and three goals down in Game 7 to end our season. There were plenty of pundits who wanted to see a complete revamping of the team, in part, I think, because the loss to Philly was so emotional. But I felt strongly that we had a solid core group of players that had come together and developed good chemistry, and I didn't want to throw that away. Still, changes had to be made.

We needed to improve our scoring, and we got the player we wanted when we traded for Nathan Horton. Gregory Campbell was an unheralded but important piece of that deal with Florida. We got two guys who could score, but the uncertainty was that both were untested in the playoffs. Our trade with Toronto netted us the second overall pick and allowed us to take Tyler Seguin, who came right in, played all season with us, and helped our speed.

Around Christmas I could tell that our team was really starting to come together, and later, as we got closer to the trade deadline, I could see that a couple of the perennial powers in the East were a little bit weaker, like Pittsburgh, which had lost Sidney Crosby and Evgeni Malkin. The timing was right. Our guys sensed it. They knew we were good. They were looking for us to make moves, and when Marc Savard went down for the year in January, we knew we needed to bring in some help.

We ended up making three significant moves before the trade deadline while we were out on a long road trip. On February 15, we did the deal for Chris Kelly with Ottawa, which is where we were headed later in the week, so he joined us there. The same day Kelly arrived, February 18, we got Rich Peverley from Atlanta and made the trade with Toronto for Tomas Kaberle, who hopped a plane and arrived at six o'clock—just an hour before game time. Those moves showed our guys that we were serious about making a run, and they responded, winning all six games on that 12-day road trip.

You have to be good to win a championship, but you also need to be lucky, and over the course of the season we had our share of bounces and calls go our way. We also stayed relatively healthy. Another key to our success was our players accepted their roles. There are always guys that feel they should be on a different line or getting in on the power play or logging more minutes—and you want players to have that drive—but we were able to come together and build momentum because everyone checked his ego at the door and did what had to be done out on the ice.

During the offseason I talked to a number of GMs, coaches, and players who have won the Cup, and I asked them about the challenges we will face in defending our title. A fellow GM likened it to climbing Mt. Everest. It's one of those things that doesn't get any easier no matter how many times you achieve it. But every person who plays for, works for, and roots for the Boston Bruins understands, respects, and appreciates what it takes to win the Stanley Cup. And we're ready to do it again.

CHAPTER ONE
PICKING UP THE PIECES

There was no way to sugarcoat it. The Bruins Game 7 collapse in their 2010 Eastern Conference semifinal matchup with the Philadelphia Flyers was historic. Only two other National Hockey League teams had ever let their opponent come back from a 3-0 deficit in a best-of-seven playoff series and as the TD Garden faithful filed out into the night after the Bruins 4-3 loss—their third straight Game 7 setback—the silence in the Bruins locker room was deafening.

As good as New England sports fans had felt after the Boston Red Sox came back from down 3-0 in 2004 to defeat the powerful New York Yankees (and the so-called Curse of the Bambino), the B's devastating loss to the "Broad Street Bullies" left Boston fans from Bangor to Bridgeport simply stunned and wondering about a new Causeway Street curse.

"I'm not going to stand here and find excuses," said Head Coach Claude Julien, who, after Game 7, was immediately thought by some pundits to be on the chopping block.[1]

"The bottom line is that we had a 3-0 lead in the series, we had a 3-0 lead [in Game 7], and we blew both," he said. "There is no excuse."[2]

To a man, the Bruins in that mausoleum-like locker room provided no excuses to the horde of hockey writers who questioned the club in the immediate aftermath of the loss. Unfortunately, no matter how many members of the Black & Gold pointed in the mirror, the 2009–10 Bruins, who had brought Boston hockey to new levels of popularity with their 2–1 overtime Winter Classic win over Philadelphia at frozen Fenway Park on New Year's Day, became one of the answers to an embarrassing trivia question thanks to those same Flyers.

General Manager Peter Chiarelli, who had navigated the B's from their DNQ playoff status after the lockout, was asked about his next steps when he spoke to the media during the club's breakup day. Chiarelli wouldn't point fingers at specific players, and wouldn't throw his coaching staff under a bus either. But the GM clearly understood the criticism he and his staff would face throughout the offseason and into the 2010–11 campaign.

1   Many outside the club felt the only logical solution was to blow the team up and start over. Not Chiarelli. "I knew we couldn't stand pat, but at the same time I couldn't overreact." Some clamored for a coaching change. "That never entered my mind," said Chiarelli. "I knew Claude would adapt and make the necessary adjustments the following season."

2   While the organization did not make any excuses for the epic collapse, it was difficult not to point to the diminished roster the Bruins featured in those final four games as the biggest factor. After Mike Richards knocked David Krejci out of the series with a dislocated wrist in Game 3, the B's depth (which was questioned before the rash of injuries) was tested even further and line combinations were again juggled. They were already without Marco Sturm (knee), Dennis Seidenberg (wrist), and Andrew Ference (groin). Marc Savard, who returned to the lineup in Game 1 against Philadelphia after missing the previous 24 games with a concussion, was not 100 percent either. This in turn forced big minutes and higher expectations on role players like Steve Begin, Vladimir Sobotka, Trent Whitfield, Blake Wheeler, and Miroslav Satan.

OPPOSITE: The reaction of the Bruins bench told the story of their Game 7 loss to the Flyers in their 2010 conference semifinal series.

"I talked to half the players this morning and these guys are shaking their heads in disbelief. They are professionals and they will move on, but there is an issue there," Chiarelli said.

Chiarelli prescribed change to assuage that "issue," but said those adjustments would be based on a pragmatic approach, not a knee-jerk reaction to a truly unthinkable end to the season.

The former Harvard Crimson hockey captain—who earned a law degree from the University of Ottawa and worked as an agent before joining the Ottawa Senators front office prior to becoming general manager of the B's in 2006—explained that his Bruins would take an academic approach in order to rebuild the shattered psyche in the Hub of Hockey and give his club another chance at hockey's Holy Grail.

"[We'll] dissect that series," said Chiarelli. "We'll look at deficiencies in our game and address them."

Instead of dwelling on the defeat, the Bruins scouting staff switched gears and headed to sunny Hollywood, the site of the 2010 NHL Entry Draft. Thanks to a September 2009 trade that sent highly touted but defensively challenged forward Phil Kessel

ABOVE: Peter Chiarelli addressed the media following the team's 2010 playoff setback.
RIGHT: Fans slumped in their seats in disbelief following Game 7, *near right*, while Zdeno Chara shakes the hand of the Flyers' Simon Gagne, *opposite page*, during the traditional post-series ritual.

to Toronto, the Bruins garnered the Leafs first and second round Entry Draft picks in 2010, as well as a first round Entry Draft pick in 2011.[3]

Happily, two can't-miss prospects, forwards Taylor Hall and Tyler Seguin, rose through the ranks during the 2009–10 junior hockey season and presented the proverbial "good problem to have" for the Edmonton Oilers. The Albertans would pick first in Los Angeles STAPLES Center to start the draft and the Bruins were slated to pick second, thanks to good fortune in the Draft Lottery.[4]

Hall, the flashier Memorial Cup champion (ironically represented by Bobby Orr's management group), was chosen by Edmonton and the B's selected Seguin, labeled a smart, well-spoken, solid player with outstanding offensive abilities and upside.[5] As such, Chiarelli sounded like a happy GM who got the player he coveted with the No. 2 pick. He called Seguin (who still retained junior hockey eligibility and would be unable to play for the AHL's Providence Bruins) "the whole package."

But how that package would fit into the B's already crowded cart was anybody's guess. In fact, the look of the Black & Gold seemed in flux as the front office had begun to assemble the 2010–11 team even in the waning moments of 2009–10.

In March, Chiarelli nabbed young University of Michigan-trained defenseman Steven Kampfer from Anaheim in a largely overlooked pre-deadline deal, and extended veteran blueliner Andrew Ference.[6] Goaltender Tim Thomas' name,

ABOVE: Tyler Seguin is greeted by the Bruins brass on stage at the 2010 NHL Entry Draft, *left to right*: Scott Bradley, Cam Neely, Charlie Jacobs, Peter Chiarelli, Seguin, Jim Benning, Wayne Smith, and Don Sweeney. TOP RIGHT: Seguin posed with Taylor Hall prior to the Entry Draft. They were ranked Nos. 1 and 2 by the NHL's Central Scouting Bureau in their final rankings. BOTTOM RIGHT: Steven Kampfer proved to be another shrewd pickup by Chiarelli.

3   The night of the Kessel trade, Mark Recchi remarked how smart of a move it was. "In the next two years we are going to have the chance to do something special," said the future Hall of Famer. "And those picks are going to be huge in helping us get there." Little did he know, that those picks would directly (drafting of Seguin) and indirectly (the Horton-Campbell trade) lead to the acquisition of key pieces to the 2011 championship puzzle.

4   Thanks to Toronto finishing with the second worst record in the league, the Bruins had a 60.8-percent chance of landing either the first or second overall pick in the 2010 Draft Lottery. Bruins management was admittedly nervous heading into the lottery, as the difference between drafting first or second overall and landing blue-chippers Hall or Seguin compared to drafting third or fourth was substantial.

5   In the days leading up to the draft, two sizable trade offers for the No. 2 overall pick landed on Chiarelli's desk, one of which involved a "significant young defenseman" and a package of picks, according to the B's GM. This offer was compelling enough to be discussed by Bruins brass at length, but while certainly intrigued, Chiarelli was never prepared to pull the trigger. Looking back on it, he believes he made the right call by holding on to the pick and tabbing Seguin.

6   Chiarelli and his scouting staff knew Anaheim had a surplus of defensemen and prospects at the time and identified Kampfer as a potential trade target. Kampfer's skill set–smart, moves well, right shot–fit what the club was looking for.

Some felt the price Chiarelli paid for Ference ($2.25 million per year for 3 years) was a little steep for a player coming off an injury-riddled season. "I feel like I'm always defending that one," said Chiarelli of the Ference contract. "But I stand by it." The B's GM felt Ference's propensity to bounce back from injury, playoff experience, and calmness on the ice was worth the cost.

bandied about in myriad trade rumors in the wake of his DNP in the playoffs and the emergence of Tuukka Rask, remained on the docket despite offers.[7] Meanwhile, Bruins beat cop Shawn Thornton and veteran forward Mark Recchi, both Stanley Cup champions, were each re-signed, as well as heavy-shot defenseman Johnny Boychuk.[8]

However, three other names were representative of the most important changes that Chiarelli would make to the team during the offseason.

Dennis Seidenberg, who was shipped to Boston with Matt Bartkowski at the 2010 trade deadline,[9] was re-signed in early June after missing the last four regular season games and all of the team's playoff games with a lacerated wrist. He was soon joined by once and future teammates Nathan Horton and Gregory Campbell later in the month as the B's sent two draft picks and much-maligned (and scapegoated) defenseman Dennis Wideman south to Sunrise.[10]

"I think it's going to be good for me and Gregory," said a very happy Horton, a certified sniper whose talents had seemed to stagnate in the South Florida sunshine.

In the meantime, Campbell, a lesser-known energy line forward who, like Horton, had never played in the Stanley Cup playoffs with the Panthers, said he had watched the 2010 postseason very closely. When asked about the B's fateful fall to the Flyers, he explained that "strange things happen" in the playoffs.

"There are so many different stories—there are so many different teams and players that step up," he added, prophetically.

Meanwhile, Chiarelli and his staff continued to pick up the pieces, but how those pieces would fit together was still to be determined as the summer sped toward 2010–11.

ABOVE: Gregory Campbell took a faceoff against Ottawa's Mike Fisher. Campbell, who came to the Bruins along with Nathan Horton in the 2010 offseason, played his first NHL playoff game in 2011, his eighth pro season. RIGHT: Dennis Seidenberg led all Boston defensemen in scoring during the 2011 playoff run.

7   With Thomas finishing the 2010 season behind Rask on the depth chart and taking up $5 million of cap space on the B's books, Bruins management and Thomas' representation met during early June to discuss the goaltender's future. During a cordial conversation, Thomas' side expressed his desire to stay in Boston and the Bruins expressed their desire to keep him, but given the goaltender's frustrating 2010 season and the Bruins salary cap situation, they also felt it would be best to see if other opportunities were out there on the trade market. However, nothing came of this mutual exploration and no trade offers were close to being considered, according to Chiarelli.

8   These three negotiations each had their own unique qualities. Thornton "might be an agent in his afterlife," said Chiarelli, noting Thornton's persuasiveness and constant banter, and the rarely seen method of involving *himself* directly in the contract talks. "That doesn't usually happen," Chiarelli mused.

    Recchi meanwhile understood the team in its current form was a contender, but would need to add a few more pieces to potentially put them over the top. He carved out a cap-friendly deal laden with playoff and performance bonuses that would fall outside the salary cap to allow the B's more flexibility. "He could have easily asked for hard money and easily gotten it elsewhere," Chiarelli recalled. "But he wanted to stay. He's a true professional in every sense of the word."

    Boychuk's negotiations began in November '09, but a deal wasn't struck until June 24, 2010. During that time, his price tag increased as he played more and his game improved, capped off by a stellar first round series against the Buffalo Sabres. "Sometimes it pays to wait, sometimes it doesn't," said Chiarelli. "He earned the pay raise."

9   The Bruins interest in Seidenberg spiked after his impressive performance against the B's in the 2009 conference semis when he was a member of the Carolina Hurricanes. That offseason, he signed a one-year deal with the Florida Panthers but became available at the 2010 trade deadline, largely because of a clause in his contract that required him to be paid $1 million on June 1 by his current team. This clause—along with the fact he was an unrestricted free agent—made him a risky acquisition as there was no guarantee he would re-sign with the team that traded for him. Chiarelli was willing to take the risk and it paid off handsomely, as Seidenberg was once again brilliant in the postseason and an unsung hero on the team's march to the championship.

10 Chiarelli had his eyes on Campbell dating back to the centerman's junior hockey days in Kitchener and tried to include him in the Seidenberg trade just four months prior. Horton was also a player Chiarelli had previously inquired about with Florida management, however the Panthers weren't willing to move him until Horton requested to be traded after the 2010 season. The key to making the Campbell-Horton deal work? Multiple first round picks. "We aren't able to make that trade unless we have two first round picks," Chiarelli said.

CHAPTER TWO

FROM CONTENDER TO CHAMPION

Amidst the signings, selections, and trades, to B's fans, the most important preseason change might have been Cam Neely's title. The Black & Gold's great No. 8 became Boston's eighth president on June 16, 2010. "The president has the responsibility for carrying the torch of the team," said Bruins Owner Jeremy Jacobs of his decision. "I can't think of a more ideal person to pass the torch to than Cam Neely."

Longtime B's fans didn't care so much about metaphorical torch passing. Instead, they wanted Neely—who combined a tremendous skill set with a ferocious approach to hockey before a hip injury cut short his on-ice career—to light a fire under the hockey pants of their beloved Bruins.

To that end, Neely said that he was excited about the direction in which the team was going, but also unequivocally stated, "I can tell you right now everybody up here is very disappointed with the way the season ended."

It was an important opening salvo from Neely, whose team's character had been questioned since mid-May. Nobody in New England was satisfied with the result of the Bruins Stanley Cup Playoff appearances since 1972 and sports talk radio was rife with opinions and predictions regarding the men who occupied the front office, ran the practices, and wore the Captain's "C" for the Black & Gold.

But instead of calming the call-in climate, Neely's elevation to the B's top spot in the front office further set the airwaves abuzz with speculation about his first order of business. Would the B's shake up the front office? Would management be more active in the free agent market? Would the Black & Gold look to make a blockbuster trade? Would Bruins players find the club's president in the locker room after games in which Neely felt as if his players had not given 100 percent?

No doubt with those heightened expectations about his possibly heavy hand in mind, Neely announced no sweeping changes to the club's boardroom. He made sure, however, to clearly state the club's singular goal was to win a sixth Stanley Cup and flatly refuted any claim that the franchise was satisfied by simply making the playoffs.

OPPOSITE: *Right to left*, Assistant GM Jim Benning, GM Peter Chiarelli, President Cam Neely, and Assistant GM Don Sweeney faced some tough questions heading into the 2010 offseason. RIGHT: Neely's importance to the organization began as a player; his No. 8 was retired by the team in January 2004.

"We're going to make everybody very proud to be a fan of the Boston Bruins," was Neely's lone prediction. Only time would tell if the Black & Gold would be able to make him into Nostradamus.

Thanks in part to well-publicized public appearances by Seguin and Horton—including an opportunity for the pair to throw out the first pitch at Fenway—the Bruins remained on the collective mind of New England's sports fans

throughout the dog days of summer. As the foliage began to turn colors, the Black & Gold returned to the B's training center at Wilmington's Ristuccia Memorial Arena and sought to turn over a new leaf in regards to the previous spring.[11]

However, in keeping with recent tradition, Chiarelli and Julien did arrange a return to the club's frequent training camp haunt of Vermont.[12] Unlike previous seasons, this trip to the Green Mountain State was a mostly private affair, devoid of public practice or media responsibilities. Instead, the team was split into groups to compete and complete delegated tasks and discuss team issues, including the club's second round series loss to Philadelphia.[13]

The longest tenured Bruin, alternate captain Patrice Bergeron, lauded the bonding exercise and explained that it was an opportunity to get to know some of the new faces that had joined the team. Moreover, Captain Chara thought

---

11   Julien put his top prospects in a position to succeed right from the start of camp, pairing Kampfer alongside Zdeno Chara and having Seguin on a line with Recchi and Patrice Bergeron for each practice and exhibition game during the preseason.

12   The Bruins had ventured to Vermont the first two years of Julien's tenure, but did not during the 2009-10 season.

13   When performing their autopsy on the 2010 season, the coaching staff identified two key areas that needed improvement in terms of the overall team dynamic: trust and accountability. Under the direction of the coaching staff and team psychologist Max Offenberger, the exercises conducted in Vermont were geared toward addressing those issues and encouraging the players to push and motivate each other.

OPPOSITE TOP: On their first visit to Boston, Nathan Horton and Tyler Seguin joined some children in the North End for a street hockey game. OPPOSITE BOTTOM: Seguin was often paired with veteran Mark Recchi in his first preseason, as Coach Julien eased the rookie into NHL life. ABOVE: As training camp neared its end, the team took time for a scenic team photo, *top*. The Bruins went to Vermont for team-building exercises.

that the Vermont trip added to the chemistry that was already growing in the perpetually close-knit Bruins locker room and also said it was an opportunity to get more deeply acquainted with how some of his teammates approached hockey as the B's prepared to round out their NHL roster.[14]

Unfortunately, concussed All-Star center Marc Savard would not be on that roster to start the 2010–11 campaign. Savard was injured by a highly questionable hit by Pittsburgh's Matt Cooke on March 7, 2010, but returned to play seven games during the B's ill-fated playoff run. He said he was still not 100 percent after a recurrence of concussion-related symptoms during the summer.[15]

"I am going to take my time and make sure I am good," Savard said. "I am just going to take it slow here."

The NHL season was coming fast and minus their most talented playmaker, the B's embarked on one more major bonding exercise as the club boarded a jet for the NHL's 2010 European tour and the beginning of the regular season.[16] Exhibition wins in Northern Ireland and the Czech Republic, as well as the mid-trip re-signing of Bergeron and Chara to

14   The theme for the trip? From Contender to Champion. "We felt the last couple of years we had become contenders," Julien said. "The next step was going from contender to champion. That's the message we wanted to deliver in Vermont."

15   Savard had reached out to Chiarelli and Communications Director Matt Chmura in early August to inform them that he may not be ready for camp and mentioned the post-concussion symptoms he was still experiencing, including depression. He came to Boston on the Bruins first day of training camp September 17 to meet with a concussion specialist and after the appointment had a private lunch with Chara, Recchi, and Marco Sturm. During an emotional exchange, he informed the players about his depression and filled them in on the difficult summer he had endured. The players told Savard that they were there to support him and also expressed their collective opinion that the best thing would be to stay around the team, so they could be there to help. With the encouragement of the players, Chiarelli, and Chmura, he would rejoin the Bruins about a week later following the team's exhibition game in Rochester, New York and began working his way back with the Bruins medical and training staff.

16   While the Vermont trip was orchestrated team building, the European trip was organic team building that occurred naturally. Players and coaches felt the two trips complemented each other well, as the players spent a lot of time getting to know each other, hanging out, and exploring the foreign cities. To a man, the Bruins believe the European trip was instrumental in their tremendous team chemistry, their trust in each other, and their overall success.

OPPOSITE: Marc Savard, pictured at a press conference with Peter Chiarelli, was unable to start the season due to lingering symptoms from a concussion suffered the previous March. TOP: The Bruins landed in Prague, Czech Republic, *left*, where they would open the season in a two-game series against Phoenix and continue their bonding process through team meals, *right*, and trips around the city. BOTTOM: Chiarelli, *right*, announced the re-signing of Patrice Bergeron while in Prague.

multiyear contracts,[17] seemingly had the B's firing on all cylinders as they prepared to take on the Phoenix Coyotes in a two-game series to start the regular season in Prague's 2010 Compuware NHL Premier games. But despite Horton's first two goals in Black & Gold, the spoked-B fell flat in the first game and lost to the Coyotes, 5–2, in O2 Arena. [18]

The following evening, Boston bounced back as Seguin scored his first NHL goal in his second NHL game.[19] Left wing Milan Lucic, injured for much of the 2009–10 campaign with a high ankle sprain, also scored his first of the season and the red-hot Horton added another tally as Thomas made 29 saves to pace the B's to a 3–0 win.

As the Bruins packed for the return trip to Boston, Head Coach Julien said that although he had enjoyed the trip to Europe, he was not sure he would have been happy with the journey had his charges returned to New England with a 0-2 record.

"It would have been a real disappointment," he said. "We came here with a purpose in mind."

Given the way Boston had overwhelmed Phoenix in the second game of the season, B's fans hoped that this "purpose" cleared customs as the club returned to the United States with 80 more games to play.

---

17   Instead of tearing the team apart after the Philadelphia series, Chiarelli did the opposite and inked his captain and alternate captain to long-term deals. From the start of negotiations, Chara and Bergeron had communicated to their agents and to Bruins management that they didn't want to play anywhere besides Boston. "I felt very strongly about staying in Boston and wanted to continue the quest I had for this team when I first signed," said Chara, who, during his introductory press conference back in 2006, explicitly stated his goal was to win a Stanley Cup in Boston. "I want to be retiring as a Boston Bruin."

18   The Chara extension was announced before the first game, and he and Chiarelli scheduled a postgame press conference to discuss the signing. After a marginal performance in the opener, the pair understandably wasn't feeling very positive as they walked from the dressing room to the press conference area. Shaking his head, Chara profusely apologized to Chiarelli for his play and the team's. Amused by how hard his captain was being on himself after just one game, Chiarelli responded with a slight smile and said, "It's a long season. We are going to have a good year, Zee, don't worry."

19   Following a team meeting that unveiled the Bruins opening day lineup, Seguin was approached by Cam Neely in the locker room hallway. "Congratulations on making it," the Hall of Famer told the 18-year-old, who just moments earlier found out he would be playing in his first NHL game. "You have a great hockey career ahead of you." The two shook hands. "I will never forget that moment for the rest of my life," Seguin recalled.

OPPOSITE TOP: Linemates David Krejci, *right*, and Nathan Horton, *left*, celebrated one of the many goals on which they collaborated, while Matt Hunwick and Mark Recchi, *center*, looked on.
OPPOSITE BOTTOM: The Bruins lined up for the opening game of the 2010–11 season in Prague's O2 Arena. ABOVE: Tyler Seguin celebrated his first NHL goal, scored against Phoenix on October 10 in Prague.

Back "Home" in Belfast

By Shawn Thornton

O ff the ice, one of the nicest moments of last season was being able to visit with my relatives in Belfast, Northern Ireland when the club stopped there on the way to the Czech Republic. Simply put, it was an awesome experience, not only for me, but also for my mother, Christine, who was born there before she moved to Canada as a young girl.

While I was there, and in the middle of us bonding as a team, I was able to reconnect with some cousins and family that I haven't seen for a long time and in some cases, ever! I have a lot of great memories of that trip, including a drive with my cousin and uncle and asking them questions about the city and the things that had happened there in the past. Then when we played the Belfast Selects, I was happy to see some familiar faces on that team; I'd played against most of them in the minors.

I also remember that trip as the time when Marchy, Soupy, and I—our "Merlot line"—really gelled as a trio, and the team started to come together for what would be our Cup run. That was my first time playing with Soupy all camp, and it was a pleasure. I got an assist on Marchy's goal that night when the puck hit me on the break out, and I heard him yelling for it, and I just chipped it to him. The rest was him.

The team had a good time out there and so did my family. During our game with the Giants, I thought everyone was going to sprain their wrists with the amount of times they waved at me, because they were so happy to be there watching me play in Northern Ireland. And I have to admit it was hard not to step back during timeouts and drink it all in from the bench. I think all the boys enjoyed that trip to Europe; it was a great time, and I don't think you can discount how instrumental that trip and the regular season trip to Vancouver was to our winning the Cup.

There's nothing wrong with it, but when you're at home everyone has their families; everyone has their lives away from the rink that occupies their time. When you're on the road for 10 or 11 days and it's just the guys, you're forced—and forced isn't a bad word in this situation—to hang out with each other every day, and you really get to know a lot about each other, which was great. It was amazing. I got to know things about guys I had played with for two or three years that I didn't know before, and I think being as close as we were was a big key in us being successful.

Personally, I would have liked another day in Belfast, but I think everyone else was pretty happy to get to Prague. It was cool. I had never been to Belfast, but to get to go and have fish and chips at the pub in my family's neighborhood, that was pretty special. To see where my mom spent the first six or seven years of her life, it was a cool experience for me. I'd always wanted to get over there, and I didn't think playing for the Bruins would be the reason that it would happen, but I'm really happy it worked out that way.

Things have often had a way of working out for me since I arrived in Boston. I'm very fortunate that my first exhibition game as a Bruin was in St. John's, where I started my career, and within my first five regular season games with Boston we went back to Anaheim and I got to see the Ducks banner go up because it was their opening night.

All in all, there are a lot of things that have kind of come together since putting on this jersey. It really makes it feel like it was meant to be the whole time.

Thanks to a five-day break that followed their European journey, the B's were well rested and ready for their first North American road games and bested both the New Jersey Devils and Washington Capitals, before they hosted the Caps for the first home game of the season on October 21.[20]

According to the players, the big news of the day was the vocal performance of the fans, who, despite the dramatic exit by their heroes in the spring, filled the TD Garden in body and sound on opening night and made sure the Black & Gold knew that New England was squarely behind their boys of winter.[21]

Chara sat in his locker postgame and talked at length about the contribution made by the TD Garden faithful to the B's 4–1 victory, which gave the Bruins their best five-game start to the season since 1990–91.

"It just shows that we have such passionate fans," said Chara. who emphatically thanked the fans for coming and being so supportive.

The Hub of Hockey would enjoy an October that saw the Bruins win six of eight, and included Thomas stopping everything in a 5–0 drubbing of the Maple Leafs on October 28. Seguin's first goal on the TD Garden ice sparked a "Thank-You-Kessel" chant from the sellout crowd that certainly reached the ears of B's former skater now toiling for the Leafs.

Thomas would later earn NHL recognition as the league's second star for the month of October as he won each of his six starts and led all goaltenders in save percentage, goals against average, and shutouts (.984, 0.50, 3)[22] en route to becoming the first Bruins goaltender to start the season 6-0-0 since Cecil "Tiny" Thompson in 1937–38. "The Tank's" highlights of the

20 The TD Garden "Bull Gang" did their part to help add some good luck to the Bruins season. When they were putting the finishing touches on the Garden ice in the preseason, they decided to freeze a penny at the center ice faceoff dot. The year on the coin? 1972, the year of the Bruins last Stanley Cup championship. That lucky penny was carved out of the ice at the end of the year and now resides in the TD Garden puck freezer, fossilized in the last remaining piece of the 2010–11 ice sheet.

The center-ice penny wasn't the only good luck charm to follow the B's around during the year. Over the summer, Chara visited a Slovakian blacksmith and picked out a horseshoe that he believed would be a fine addition to the Bruins locker room at home and on the road. The horseshoe features seven holes, which was odd since most horseshoes have an even number. "Lucky Seven," thought Chara. He also felt it was fitting given the importance of the number seven in postseason play. He packed the horseshoe in his luggage on his flight from Slovakia to Boston and had the Bruins equipment staff secure it to a wooden board so that it could easily be hung above the TD Garden locker room doorway. Chara and the Bruins players would tap the horseshoe with their sticks on their way out of the dressing room.

21 The Bruins would go on to sell out every TD Garden home game during the 2010–11 season, finishing the year on a 71-game sellout streak (84 including playoffs).

22 Those gaudy numbers weren't good enough for First Star honors, as the NHL gave the nod to Tampa's Steven Stamkos (19 points on 9 goals and 10 assists in 10 games).

OPPOSITE: Coach Julien gave instruction to the players on the Bruins bench during a timeout.

month also included 73 saves in two wins over Washington and back-to-back shutout victories over Ottawa and Toronto.[23]

Offseason hip surgery was key to the puckstopper's revival.[24]

"There's definitely a difference in my capability," explained Thomas, who took home the Vezina Trophy in 2009 before losing the starting job to rookie goalie Tuukka Rask in 2009–10. "Now, it's up to me to bring that capability and do the job when I get the chance."[25]

Despite Thomas' Bruins-best 7-0-0 start to the season and a stirring five-goal third period versus Pittsburgh on November 10, which saw the B's climb out of a two-goal third-period hole to beat the Penguins 7–4,[26] the club faltered in November, going just 6-6-2. One highlight during this stretch was Milan Lucic's second career hat trick on November 18 against Florida.[27] The Black & Gold were then buoyed by the return of Savard (who had missed the first 23 games of the campaign) on December 2, when the spoked-B garnered an 8–1 victory over the Tampa Bay Lightning.

ABOVE: Tim Thomas posed at the NHL Awards in Las Vegas with his first Vezina Trophy. RIGHT: Marc Savard returned to the ice for his first game of the season on December 2 versus Tampa Bay.

23 Julien held a closed-door meeting with both Thomas and Rask in September and reiterated what he told Thomas during his exit interview back in May 2010. Julien said he believed the Bruins had the best goaltender tandem in the league and that just because Rask finished the 2010 season between the pipes, he wasn't going to be handed the starting goaltender job, he would have to earn it. "There is no No. 1 goalie to start the season," he told his netminders. "But that's a positive thing, not a negative. You are both going to get the opportunity and we will ride whoever has the hot hand." Thomas certainly had the hot hand to start the year and earned the bulk of the work. However Rask, who would prove to be invaluable later in the season, played well while giving Thomas the chance for much-needed rest to gear up for the postseason run.

24 The day after the surgery, Thomas immediately knew something had changed in his hip for the better. And over the course of the summer his confidence returned. When he hit the ice for the first time in late August he experienced some discomfort, but his doctors told him this was normal and it would take about two weeks before the pain subsided. By the time Thomas began working with Bruins Goaltender Coach Bob Essensa at the beginning of training camp, the pain had gone away as his doctors predicted. And as the preseason proceeded, his confidence continued to grow. He was 100-percent pain-free "for the first time in a long time" during his first start of the regular season on October 10.

25 Thomas also credits his Accelerated Recovery and Performance (ARP) machine for his quick rehabilitation and condition. Brought to his attention by Team USA teammate Zach Parise during the 2010 Olympics, the ARP machine is a box-like unit with dials, a timer, and wires that attach to pads placed on the body. Low-voltage electrical currents shoot into the body during workouts and help to reduce recovery time and heal sore muscles and joints.

26 This five-goal outburst in the third period against a healthy Penguins squad is one game that many Bruins personnel point to as a key moment during the season. "It helped us understand what we were capable of and helped us understand we were never out of it," Julien said. "We were a 'no-quit' kind of team."

27 In his "picture with the pucks" Lucic is sporting a gray fedora signed by the Bruins team. The hat's original owner? Brad Marchand. Marchand frequently wore the hat in the weeks leading up to this game and was incessantly ribbed by his teammates, who weren't particularly fond of it or how it looked on him. Before their game against the Devils on November 15, Marc Savard—who was among the more outspoken critics of the hat—placed it on the team's autograph table with a sharpie (if a player wants something signed by the team they will  place the item on this table). Usually the items placed on this table are Bruins sticks or jerseys, but Recchi saw the hat and autographed it, assuming that Marchand put it there and wanted it signed. One by one, the rest of the team followed and by the end of the game, it was now a fully signed team hat. Marchand found the whole situation humorous and even though he wouldn't wear the hat publicly again, it stayed in the TD Garden locker room for the remainder of the season.

ABOVE TOP: Goaltender Tim Thomas checked out the action on his stickside. ABOVE BOTTOM: Between Tuukka Rask and Thomas, a Boston goaltender has had the league's top goals against average and save percentage in each of the last three seasons. LEFT: Mark Recchi, *left*, and Marc Savard celebrated after Recchi's goal, which helped spark a comeback win over the Penguins on January 10, 2011.

"The fans were fantastic," the center said of the prolonged standing ovation in the TD Garden. "I got a little emotional there...it was special."[28]

Even more special was the B's 8-3-3 record in December, a month that saw defenseman Andrew Ference score his first goal in 100 games and Thomas make 25 saves in the third period alone in a 3-2 win over Washington on December 18.[29] December also witnessed Thornton, the B's resident tough guy, score two goals during a December 23 contest versus Atlanta that featured a Big Bad Bruins-style line brawl in the third period.[30]

The Bruins rang in 2011 with a 7-4-2 record in January, but pulled out another win over Pittsburgh thanks to four goals in the final 3:33 to win 4–2 on January 10, just two nights after the B's squandered their own 2–0 lead with under three minutes to go against Montreal to lose 3–2 in overtime.[31] This two-game sequence against the hated Habs and the Penguins demonstrated the emotional peaks and valleys Bruins fans experienced throughout the 2010–11 season. The Bruins followed up an improbable third-period collapse in one of their worst losses of the year, with an improbable third-period comeback in one of their most memorable wins.

Back at home the following evening, in the B's 42nd game of the season, Bergeron began the second half with his first career hat trick in a 6–0 win over Ottawa.

The Flyers visited the Garden on January 13 and played in one of the more entertaining regular season games of the season on Causeway Street. The clubs saw a combined 12 different goal scorers, two-point performances by six different members of the Black & Gold, and six lead changes. Kampfer notched the game-winner with 1:14 remaining and Campbell scored an empty net goal—the seventh goal scored in the third period—to make the final 7–5 Bruins.

ABOVE: Zdeno Chara, Patrice Bergeron, and Blake Wheeler listened to Coach Julien during a timeout. OPPOSITE TOP: Chara received congratulations from the B's bench after a Bruins goal. OPPOSITE MIDDLE: Brad Marchand beat Pittsburgh's Marc-Andre Fleury for the tying goal in a January comeback win over the Penguins. OPPOSITE BOTTOM: The Bruins energy line of Shawn Thornton, *center*, Daniel Paille, *left*, and Gregory Campbell, *right*, on the ice after one of Thornton's two goals against the Thrashers on December 18.

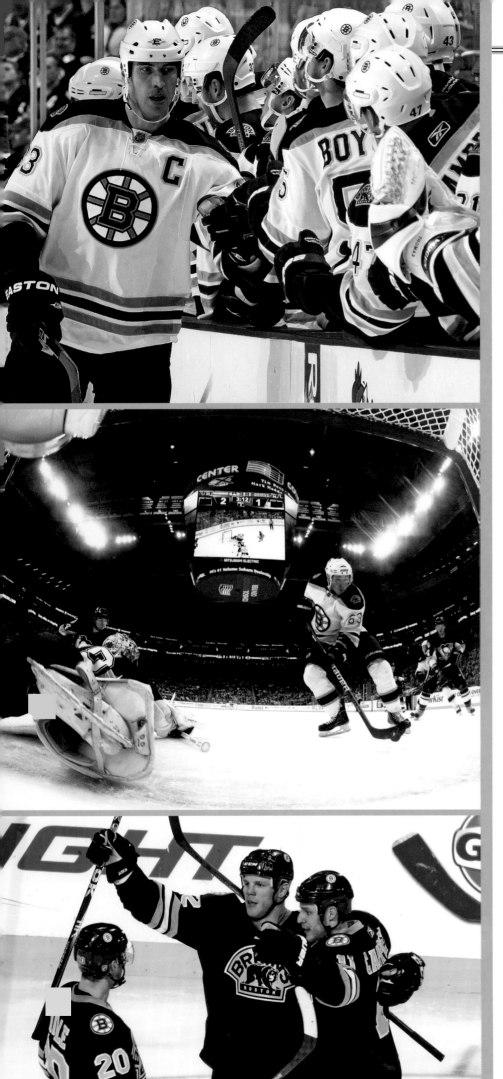

28   After he spoke publicly about his depression, Savard began receiving hundreds and hundreds of letters offering support and words of encouragement. Some wrote to say they had experienced similar problems and emphasized that he wasn't alone in his battle, while others just wrote to wish him well. He was truly appreciative of the people who took the time to write. Reading their letters was very therapeutic for him.

29   Veteran Marco Sturm–who secured his place in Bruins lore for his game-winning strikes in the "this-building-is-vibrating" game against the Canadiens in 2008 and the Winter Classic at Fenway Park in 2010–was sent west to Los Angeles for future considerations on December 11. Despite not receiving a player or a pick in return, this was a move that benefitted both the Bruins and Sturm: the Bruins received much needed cap relief by shedding his salary, while Sturm was able to join a team that gave him an opportunity to play.

30   After dropping three of four–including a lackluster 3–0 defeat against the Ducks on home ice–Julien put the Bruins through two days of intense, physical practices leading up to this game. To establish the tone early, he rolled out his energy line to kick off the contest. Thornton immediately jumpstarted the game by taking on Thrasher tough guy Eric Boulton as soon as the puck dropped. The two engaged in an entertaining bout that set the table for the rest of the evening. With his parents in attendance, Thornton would enjoy one of the best games of his career, scoring two goals (and nearly had a third after ringing a post) in addition to the scrap. Hoping for an improbable hat trick from their favorite fourth liner, the TD Garden crowd chanted Thornton's name in the third period and even booed when his shifts ended. "One of the best hockey moments of my life," said Thornton of the fan support. "Growing up you dream about that, a whole building chanting your name. That was pretty special."

31   In between the loss to the Canadiens and the win over the Pens, the coaching staff held a full team meeting on Sunday, January 9, at their hotel in Pittsburgh, where they addressed the poor decision making and mistakes that cost them the game the previous night at the Bell Centre. The point of emphasis during this meeting? Playing a *full 60 minutes*. "The Montreal game was a valuable learning experience for the team," Julien said. "It was nice to see that within two games we reversed a trend."

The B's headed west for matchups with Colorado and Los Angeles, but the short trip would prove costly as Matt Hunwick, traded by the Bruins to the Mile High City on November 29,[32] laid a hit that concussed Savard in the B's 6–2 win over the Avalanche on January 22 and ended the center's season after just 25 games.[33]

To round out January, Boston sent three participants to the NHL All-Star festivities in Raleigh, North Carolina. Seguin participated in the SuperSkills competition and Chara set a new record with a 105.9 mph blast—shattering his old mark of 105.4 mph that he set in 2009—en route to his fourth consecutive Hardest Shot title.[34] But it was Thomas who stole the show when he fell rounding the net during his race with Carolina Hurricanes goaltender Cam Ward as part of the Fastest Skater competition.

Despite what could have been an embarrassing moment, the NHL veteran handled it with a smile and a few laughs and bounced back the next day to become the first NHL goalie ever to win three consecutive All-Star games as Team Lidstrom defeated Team Staal 11–10 to end the unofficial first half of 2010–11.

32 Hunwick was deemed expendable because the Bruins needed to clear cap space with Savard and Marco Sturm coming off Long Term Injured Reserve and B's management saw Kampfer emerge as a less expensive, but very capable replacement with a similar skill package.

33 While Savard was shut down after the Hunwick collision, the Bruins believe Deryk Engellend's hit on Savard (which was clean) in the third period of a 3–2 home loss to the Pens on January 15 also contributed.

34 During this contest, Chara quickly realized how serious the other participants were taking it, as some of the competitors were skating in from the red line to build up more speed (standard Hardest Shot rules have the participants start from the blue line). When he advanced to the Final, he and Nashville's Shea Weber agreed to both start from the blue line. Weber had the better of the Chara in the opening round with a competition-best 104.8 mph (Chara felt he was trying to overpower everything in the first round). But on his record-setting shot in the Final, Chara said he "relaxed, and let the stick swing."

OPPOSITE TOP: Zdeno Chara took the ice at the 2011 All-Star Game in Raleigh, North Carolina. OPPOSITE BOTTOM: Chara broke his own record while winning his fourth straight Hardest Shot competition with a 105.9 mph blast. ABOVE: Tim Thomas became the first goalie ever to win three straight NHL All-Star games.

CHAPTER FOUR
MAKING MOVES

G

oing into the NHL's annual swap and shop, nobody in the Black & Gold locker room wanted to be traded, but it seemed inevitable that the B's would make some moves down the stretch.[35]

Despite what was seen as a statement game versus the Dallas Stars on February 3—a contest that featured 91 minutes in penalties, three fights in the first four seconds of play (Campbell vs. Steve Ott, Thornton vs. Krys Barch, and Adam McQuaid vs Brian Sutherby),[36] and nine points for the line of Bergeron (2 goals, 1 assist), surprising rookie agitator Brad Marchand (1 goal, 2 assists), and Recchi (3 assists) in a 6–3 Boston win—the Bruins started the NHL's unofficial second half with some subpar hockey.

A 2–0 loss to San Jose on February 5 (the first-ever shutout by the Sharks over Boston) was the first sign that the B's might have to make some changes if they wanted to be able to test the mettle of the Western Conference. And while an 8–6 Bruins win over the Montreal Canadiens on February 9 might have been entertaining—182 total penalty minutes and a short pugilistic soiree at center ice between the Habs Carey Price and the B's Thomas[37]—it was hardly indicative of a B's team that was ready to challenge for Eastern Conference supremacy.

However, it was the Bruins two defeats against the Detroit Red Wings on February 11 (6–1 in Boston) and February 13 (4–2 in Detroit)[38] and the club's heartbreaking 4–3 loss to the Maple Leafs in Boston (in which Toronto scored twice in the last 6:33 of the game) that seemed certain to stimulate a shakeup

Following the game against the Leafs on February 15, Boston announced the acquisition of forward Chris Kelly from the Ottawa Senators for a second round pick.[39]

The B's started an important six-game road swing on February 17 and kicked things off with a 6–3 win over the New York Islanders, a victory that featured a goal and an assist each from Lucic, Seguin, Krejci, and Blake Wheeler.

[35] There is a running not-so-funny joke around the Bruins: Hang out with Shawn Thornton, prepare to pack your bags. A laundry list of players including Glen Metropolit, Jeremy Reich, P.J. Axelsson, Aaron Ward, and Shane Hnidy (during his first Bruins tour) were all running mates of Thornton that had moved on to other teams since Thornton began his own tenure with the Bruins in 2007.

Early in 2011, during his weekly call-in with *The Toucher and Rich Show*, Thornton was hounded by the hosts for habitually driving to practice and hanging out with popular defenseman Mark Stuart (who was actually in the car with Thornton at the time of the call) and implied that if "Stuey" were moved at the NHL's deadline it would be Thornton's fault.

[36] With the exception of the Campbell-Ott tilt, the Bruins earned one-sided unanimous decisions in the three other fights. Barch required surgery to repair a broken orbital bone on his face thanks to Thornton, but perhaps most impressive was the 5'11", 189-pound Andrew Ference's dismantling of the 6'1", 200-pound Adam Burish. Like Barch, Burish also needed surgery to repair a broken orbital bone, however he had to wait nearly a week for the swelling on his face to subside before he could safely be operated on.

[37] This was the first altercation of Thomas' career that involved another goalie. He has had his fair share of pushing and shoving with forwards (Sean Avery, Andrei Kostitsyn, and Henrik Sedin just to name a few) but his throwdown with Price was the first of its kind. His inexperience showed as the two netminders grappled momentarily and tumbled to the ice. What made this even more entertaining was the fact that Thomas and Price are friendly off the ice.

[38] While navigating the corridors of Joe Louis Arena after the loss in Detroit on February 13, Chiarelli decided it was time to shake things up. "I felt we were in a bit of malaise, I needed to get us on the board and get a deal done," Chiarelli said. He had a trade teed up with Ottawa for centerman Chris Kelly, a player with whom he had a history, and believed the time was right.

[39] Chiarelli had worked on the Kelly deal for months, however he was initially uncomfortable with Ottawa's asking price—a second round pick. In the Sens mind, the second round pick was non-negotiable, and they didn't budge on what they wanted in return for the 30-year-old centerman from the start of the negotiations through the completion. "When you go into the trade market ahead of the deadline, the prices are high," remarked Chiarelli. "The price for Kells did not change and was not going to change had we waited."

OPPOSITE: New names and faces were added to the Boston Bruins locker room during the second half of the 2010–11 regular season.

It would be Wheeler's last points with the Bruins as he and Stuart were both dealt to the Atlanta Thrashers the following day[40] in a deal that saw forward Rich Peverley join Boston. Then, prospect Joe Colborne and two draft picks were sent to Toronto in exchange for defenseman Tomas Kaberle,[41] a puck-moving power play expert who was meant to inject some life into the Bruins man-advantage unit.

The next night, February 18, Kaberle and Kelly (in front of his former home crowd) made their Bruins debut in a 4–2 win over Ottawa that saw Marchand score a pair. The B's continued their Canadian tour in Calgary with a 3–1 win on February 22, thanks to two goals from Lucic and 28 saves from a well-rested Thomas. Four nights later, Lucic continued his own personal revival when he notched a goal and two assists in a 3–1 Bruins win over his hometown Vancouver Canucks[42]—just one night after his junior club, the Vancouver Giants, inducted him into the Giants Ring of Honour during "Milan Lucic" night in the Pacific Coliseum.

The Bruins continued their remarkable road trip with a 3–2 win in Edmonton on February 27 courtesy of Peverley, whose first goal as a Bruin was the game-winner. The following night, Rask[43] finished the trip with a 33-save shutout in a Horton-fueled 1–0 win over the Sens to give the Bruins their first perfect six-game road trip since 1972.[44]

ABOVE TOP LEFT: Forward Milan Lucic scored the game-winner in his hometown of Vancouver during the club's pivotal February road swing. ABOVE BOTTOM LEFT: Forward Chris Kelly began his Bruins career versus Ottawa, just three days after being acquired from the Senators. ABOVE RIGHT: Goaltender Tuukka Rask made a save during the Bruins 3-2 win versus the Oilers in Edmonton. OPPOSITE: Puck-moving defenseman Tomas Kaberle was acquired by Boston from Toronto in exchange for prospect Joe Colborne and two draft picks.

40 After the pregame meal in Ottawa, road roommates Krejci and Wheeler headed up to their room to rest up before the evening's game. Shortly after they settled in, Wheeler's cell phone rang. The name and number that popped up on the screen was not the one he hoped to see—it was Peter Chiarelli. "This can't be good," thought Wheeler before he answered. Sure enough, Chiarelli delivered the news—Wheeler was no longer a Boston Bruin.

41 The Kelly, Peverley, and Kaberle trades were all highly intertwined. After Kelly was acquired, the Peverley trade needed to happen next in order to clear enough cap space to bring in Kaberle, but Chiarelli wasn't going to do the Peverley deal unless he was certain the Kaberle trade would go through. "We knew Savvy wasn't coming back so we needed some more depth at forward," said the Bruins GM. "I felt we were a good team with a chance to win. It was important for us to get these deals done early in the game." Looking at these three trades together, the Bruins cleared cap space (by moving Stuart) and received two forwards (Kelly and Peverley) for one (Wheeler) in return. This two-for-one trade gave the Bruins the kind of depth up front they had lacked the prior year.

42 Players, coaches, and management all point to this road trip as a key juncture in the championship season. Not only did they win all six games—including two complete 60-minute performances against the then-streaking Calgary Flames and red-hot Vancouver Canucks—but they became closer as a team. Three off-days in Vancouver provided the opportunity for the new acquisitions to get to know their new teammates away from the rink. The B's had a full team dinner (their first since Prague) and were able to relax and hang out away from the rink. Had Chiarelli waited until the deadline to act on the trades he was contemplating, the team bonding that took place on this road trip could have not happened.

43 It's easy to forget that during this vital road trip, Rask won four of the six decisions. After the All-Star break, Julien made a concerted effort to increase Rask's workload in order to rest up Thomas to prepare his No. 1 goaltender for the stretch run. From February 17 through March 17, Thomas played only in six of the team's 13 games.

44 It was clear to see how well the group got along aboard the team charter, lightheartedly referred to as "Bear Force One." Walking down the aisle of the plane—which was the same plane U2 used on a recent tour—you'd see Rask, Boychuk, Peverley, Ryder, and Marchand huddled around the card table playing Schnarpps; Horton, Lucic, and Ference passing their iPad back-and-forth entrenched in an intense game of Scrabble; Krejci, Seguin, and Kampfer playing *Call of Duty* on Xbox (they couldn't leave their belongings on the plane after every road trip so Kampfer's carry-on item each flight was the TV monitor, Krejci's was the Xbox); and the Bergeron-Paille and Chara-Seidenberg rows watching movies together. Meanwhile, Thornton and Recchi had their own area in the back of the plane that they named the "Three Rings Lounge," (in reference to Recchi's two Cup rings and Thornton's one) complete with a Three Rings Lounge sign, music, and table (Kaberle would join them after he was acquired). The trio joked that they would hopefully have to update the name of the lounge after the season and call it "Six Rings Lounge."

Despite a four-game losing streak following the road trip, there were plenty of memorable moments for the Bruins as the final days of 2010–11 campaign sped Boston toward the Stanley Cup playoffs.

Beyond stopping a season-worst losing skid on March 15,[45] Peverley scored one of most memorable goals of the regular season on a brilliant shorthanded tally against the Columbus Blue Jackets with six minutes remaining in the game. His goal tied the contest at 2–2 and set up a Seguin shootout winner that gave the B's their 2,800th win as a franchise. It also marked Recchi's 1,640th game, which moved him into fifth place on the NHL's all-time list.[46]

The Bruins downed the Canadiens 7–0 on March 24 to put the club five points up on Montreal with nine games remaining in the regular season.[47] Thanks to Marchand's 20th goal,[48] the B's then clinched a fourth-straight playoff berth on March 27 with a 2–1 win at Philadelphia, and locked up the Northeast Division with a 3–2 victory over Atlanta on April 2.

Off the ice, the fourth annual 98.5 The Sports Hub & Shawn Thornton Cuts for a Cause event was held on April 7 and raised $42,722.35 for the Boston Bruins Foundation and Floating Hospital for Children at Tufts Medical Center.[49] This was the last of the Bruins' many charitable and community events the team participated in before the end of the season.

ABOVE: Forward Rich Peverley was traded to Boston from the Thrashers in a deal that saw defenseman Mark Stuart and forward Blake Wheeler head to Atlanta. OPPOSITE TOP: Veteran forward Mark Recchi's leadership was integral to the Bruins transformation from contender to champion. OPPOSITE MIDDLE: Rookie forward Brad Marchand, *right*, began the season playing on the B's energy line. OPPOSITE BOTTOM: Shawn Thornton posed with a pediatric patient during the fourth annual Cuts for a Cause event.

45 Bergeron called a players-only meeting before the B's morning skate at Nationwide Arena on March 15. Having just lost four in a row to the Penguins, Canadiens, Sabres, and the bottom-dwelling Islanders, Bergeron sensed some frustration amongst the ranks and felt the need to step up and address the group. Imploring his teammates to go out and have some fun instead of squeezing their sticks and getting frustrated, Bergeron said, "Realize how lucky we are to be playing the game we love for a living and go out there and enjoy it." Known more for being a leader-by-example as opposed to an outspoken type, this was an instance where Bergeron felt being vocal was what the team needed.

46 The surefire Hall of Famer ended his NHL regular season career with 1,652 games played (fourth all-time), 577 goals (19th all-time), and 956 assists (13th all-time) for 1,533 points (12th all-time).

47 The stakes were almost as high as the tension in this one, with the teams only separated by three points in the Northeast Division standings entering the game. It was also the first matchup between the two squads since Max Pacioretty was injured when he collided with a stanchion in between the two benches on March 8.

48 Marchand's "20-goal guarantee" during his 2010 offseason meeting with Julien and Chiarelli sums up the type of confidence and swagger the 23-year-old carries with him. During that meeting with Julien in which they reviewed the previous year, the coach told him that in the 20 games he played that year, his confidence diminished as the games went on. Bruins management felt like he could do better and there were some changes he needed to make. Julien went on to say they would be happy with Marchand being a 4th-line player who would get 10 goals a year and bring a lot of energy to the game. Marchand took that as an opportunity to sell himself. He expressed how badly he wanted to be on the team in 2010–11 and told him "the more comfortable I get in the league, I can be a 20-goal scorer." He easily captured the team's 7th Player Award for his breakout performance in 2011, for performing above and beyond expectations of Bruins fans.

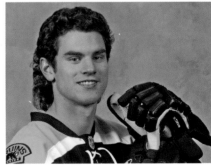

49 Nicknamed "Darth Quaider," McQuaid was the star at Cuts for a Cause. Instead of shaving his head, McQuaid's teammates and the fans in attendance convinced him to style his hair into a mullet, which drew rave reviews. Teammate Andrew Ference had made T-shirts up with a Darth Vader *Star Wars* mask sporting a mullet, with the words "Darth Quaider" arching above.

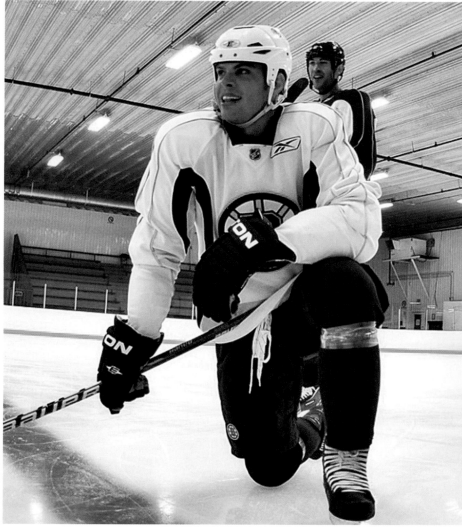

Thomas and Lucic enjoyed big days at home against Ottawa on April 9, as Lucic notched his 30th goal of the season and Thomas closed out his regular season renaissance with an NHL record setting .938 save percentage[50] and led the league in goals against average (2.00). Chara ended the season with a league leading plus-33, despite being deployed against the opposition's most dangerous scoring line night in and night out and logging the most minutes on the team. But nobody in the B's locker room sounded satisfied with a Northeast Division Championship as the Black & Gold prepared for the first round of the Stanley Cup playoffs.

Their first round opponent? The Montreal Canadiens.

"This is what you play for as a hockey player," said Horton of the B's first round matchup with Montreal. "To be in this situation and be involved in it is pretty special."

50   The hockey tradition of putting "money on the board" (when players put a sum of money on the locker room whiteboard before a game, and if the team wins, that player owes that amount to the team fund) is usually reserved for when a player battles a former team or plays a game on the road in his hometown (for example, if the Bruins played the Canadiens, Ryder may put $500 on the board since he used to play for them). However, because Thomas knew he needed to surrender two or fewer goals in his last regular season start against Ottawa to break the NHL save percentage record, he put $5,000 (a high amount, unusual to see anyone put over $1,000) on the board for a "two-goals-against-or-fewer" performance. Sure enough, the Bruins only allowed one and Thomas finished with a .938 save percentage, breaking Dominik Hasek's old record of .937.

OPPOSITE: Drafted by the Florida Panthers, Nathan Horton's move north to Boston left the forward smiling as he looked forward to playing his first NHL playoff game in his eighth pro season. ABOVE: Captain Zdeno Chara tapped helmets with Tim Thomas after a late-season win.

Vintage Memories

By Andrew Ference

Sometimes memories come cheap—50 bucks including shipping in the case of our team jacket. Late last February I completed a month-long search for some vintage Bruins apparel when I found a "Chalkline" brand Bruins jacket circa early '80s on eBay. It was a personal purchase, so I could wear something fun around the locker room before games. But it soon turned into a "reward" for a player who had a particularly good performance. It was expected that the player would wear it for all media interviews after the game and then be responsible for passing it out after the next win.

The jacket's first public appearance was on Milan Lucic after he reached the 30-goal mark late in the season, and it soon found its way around the room as the wins were plenty and as different guys stepped up their games each night. The tradition carried on into the playoffs, and with each passing round, our ceremony after a win became a nice way for the coach to say a few words and the boys to have a good laugh at the expense of the jacket recipient. The most significant moment of this jacket's life started with Nathan Horton's Game 7 goal against Tampa Bay. After that game he was awarded the jacket, and because of our Vancouver losses he held onto it through Game 3 of the Final. We all know about his injury in that game, and after the win he was at the hospital for tests and obviously unable to pass on the jacket. Coach Julien asked Zee and me after the game if we thought it was a good idea not to give it out but to wait for Nathan to do it when he was able. I think everyone was already thinking along the same lines, which made the decision easy—nobody would get the jacket until it could be properly passed out by the current custodian.

As if a massive Game 4 win was not emotional enough, after we were all gathered in the room Coach told us it was time to pass out the jacket and Horty walked into the room with it, and the guys went nuts! Even in the chaos that followed Game 7, we all found a moment after everyone else was kicked out of the room to have a chat and pass out the jacket one last time. Gregory Campbell gave it to Mark Recchi, who I think was about the perfect guy to wear it one last time. Oh yeah, the eBay user I bought it from, "fasinfrankvintage," is from Vancouver.

The Jacket Tally:

REGULAR SEASON
3/22 vs. NJ: Milan Lucic
3/24 vs. MTL: Zdeno Chara
3/27 at PHI: Tim Thomas
3/29 vs. CHI: Mark Recchi
4/2 vs. ATL: Tuukka Rask
4/6 vs. NYI: Daniel Paille
4/9 vs. OTT: Rich Peverley

STANLEY CUP PLAYOFFS
4/18 at MTL, Game 3: Patrice Bergeron
4/21 at MTL, Game 4: Michael Ryder
4/23 vs. MTL, Game 5: Tim Thomas
4/27 vs. MTL, Game 7: Nathan Horton

4/30 at PHI, Game 1: David Krejci
5/2 at PHI, Game 2: Tim Thomas
5/4 vs. PHI, Game 3: Dennis Seidenberg
5/6 vs. PHI, Game 4: Milan Lucic

5/17 vs. TB, Game 2: Tyler Seguin
5/19 at TB, Game 3: Tim Thomas
5/23 vs. TB, Game 5: Chris Kelly
5/27 vs. TB, Game 7: Nathan Horton

6/8 vs. VAN, Game 3: (was not passed out)
6/10 vs. VAN, Game 4: Rich Peverley
6/13 vs. VAN, Game 6: Gregory Campbell
6/15 at VAN, Game 7: Mark Recchi

CHAPTER FIVE

NO REGRETS

EASTERN CONFERENCE
QUARTERFINAL

Boston fans find themselves in the middle of many pivotal, pulse-pounding, intense rivalries: Red Sox vs. Yankees, Celtics vs. Lakers, and, of course, Bruins vs. Canadiens.

There's no more purely intense competition on the ice than *bleu, blanc et rouge* vs. Black & Gold, and the tumultuous 2010–11 season just added to the history of hatred between the two venerable Original Six franchises. That said, since the B's began the all-time series with the Habs on December 8, 1924, the rivalry was often a one-sided affair as the Bruins held a meager 8-24 record in 32 postseason series.

But it was a contest on March 8, which sharpened the edge of the antagonism between the clubs. Chara, who had confronted Montreal's Pacioretty earlier in the season as he celebrated an overtime game-winner on January 8, was involved in a controversial on-ice collision with Pacioretty and the stanchion in between the two benches. This left the Montreal winger severely injured and had incited calls for NHL (and even provincial) discipline.[51]

Chara was given no supplemental discipline and NHL Senior Vice President Mike Murphy said, "This was a hockey play that resulted in an injury because of the player colliding with the stanchion and then the ice surface."

The Habs and their fans didn't see it that way and, while Pacioretty remained sidelined throughout the playoffs, the B's presence in Quebec heightened the already hostile environments in both Montreal's Bell Centre and Boston's TD Garden.

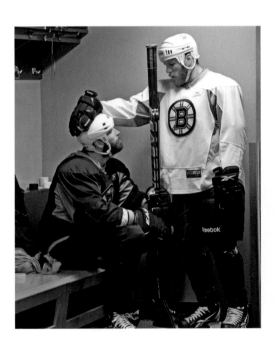

51   Chara called a rare team meeting in the visitor's locker room of the Air Canada Centre before their morning skate in Toronto on March 19. "The Montreal police are going to open an investigation and they may talk to you about it," the captain informed his 23 teammates and coaches. "I don't want it to be a distraction for the team. I will handle it." This was a moment where the team rallied around their captain and helped him through what could have been a difficult distraction to put aside.

OPPOSITE: David Krejci took a faceoff against Montreal's Tomas Plekanec.

NO REGRETS CHAPTER FIVE   67

Full 60+ to History Explained

by Claude Julien

Since taking over the Bruins coaching reigns in 2007, I have worked with the Bruins marketing group and Graphic Designer Jason Petrie to create motivational posters for the playoffs that become part of the team's postgame meeting after each playoff win. These special posters are meant to show the progress the club has made, but also show our players how far they still need to go to reach their ultimate goal of winning the Stanley Cup.

We put a lot of effort into this motivational tool, and, like our team-building trips at the beginning of the fall, as a coaching staff we like to do something a little different and a little unique every spring.

In 2010, for example, our poster took on the *Survivor* TV-show theme of "Outsmart, Outwork, Outlast," and after each series was clinched, the Stanley Cup graphic (which we broke down into four parts) would fill up. The previous year, in the spring of 2009, the theme was "16 Steps," and after each win the logo of the team we defeated would be placed on the next step.

It sounds simple, but I've seen it become a useful coaching tool over the years. So last March, after we clinched a playoff spot, I told Petrie that we wanted this year's concept to focus on playing the "Full 60 Minutes," a theme we had emphasized as a coaching staff—even harped on—to the team throughout the season.

The first idea to come to Petrie was incorporating some sort of timing device, so he went to work and came up with an old-style stopwatch design that was divided into 16 different triangular pie pieces. After each win, the First Star of the game—or in this case, the recipient of the Bruins jacket that Andy Ference brought into the locker room—could stick a pie piece featuring the opposing team's logo on the poster, and it would fill up as we progressed through the playoffs.

Understanding how important playing the full 60 minutes was to winning, as well as knowing the historical significance of a Stanley Cup victory and what the Cup would mean to our city, Petrie came up with the slogan "Full 60 to Victory, Full 60 to History" and showed me his design. I immediately liked the idea, but I think I also raised a fair question. "What if we go to overtime?" I asked.

And that is why the plus sign was added.

Every day, looking at the poster hanging in the locker room, the players were constantly reminded that it would take a full 60-minute effort, and even more than that if the game went into OT, in order to achieve our goals. So along with handing out the jacket, adding another pie piece to the stopwatch poster became a playoff postgame tradition that the team truly enjoyed and I enjoyed watching.

When Mark Recchi placed the fourth and final Vancouver Canuck piece on the poster after Game 7 of the Final—a game in which EVERY member of our team contributed a full 60-minute effort—our team realized we didn't merely achieve victory on that night.

We made history.

W.I.N.

4 5 6 7 8 9 10 11 12 13 14 15 16

BRUINS
BOSTON
PLAYOFFS 2009

FULL 60+
TO VICTORY

FULL 60+
TO HISTORY

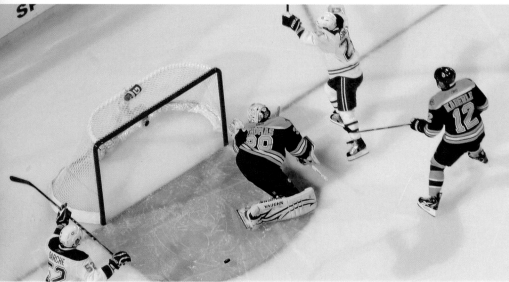

GAME 1 APRIL 14, 2011[52]

MONTREAL 2 BOSTON 0

ormer Boston College standout Brian Gionta, who had played Hockey East playoff and Beanpot games for the Eagles at the TD Garden, returned to tournament action on Causeway Street and revived his collegiate heroics in the Eastern Conference quarterfinals when he scored the only two goals of the contest.

Meanwhile, at the other end of the ice, Montreal's Carey Price stopped all 31 shots he saw for his third career playoff shutout.

"Every game is a different story, sometimes you get the bounces and sometimes you don't; playoffs especially, everyone comes to battle every night," said Marchand postgame. "I think they're all going to be one, two-goal games.

"You have to be prepared for that."

---

52   There was an immense amount of pressure put on the Bruins to perform well in this postseason from the outside (that's to be expected when you don't win a championship in 39 years). Some believed that the Bruins needed to advance past the second round in order for Julien to keep his job, others felt a disappointing first round loss would mean a full housecleaning. The team did an outstanding job insulating themselves from this pressure and blocking out the negative consequences an early playoff exit would potentially bring. "I couldn't let the outside stuff affect the team or myself at all," Julien said. "I had to brush that all aside and told our guys to relax, stay positive, and be determined."

OPPOSITE TOP: Coach Julien addressed the team at the morning skate prior to the opening game of the postseason. OPPOSITE BOTTOM: Montreal's Brian Gionta celebrated one of his two goals against Tim Thomas in Game 1 of the series. ABOVE: Milan Lucic went airborne in an effort to get a shot on Montreal's Carey Price.

GAME 2 APRIL 16, 2011
MONTREAL 3 BOSTON 1

Despite Marchand's prediction, the B's simply looked unprepared for the second game of the series as Montreal's Michael Cammalleri scored just 43 seconds into the first period and Mathieu Darche beat Thomas for a power play goal just a minute and 37 seconds later.

Boston's slow start surely had much to do with the fact that Chara was hospitalized for dehydration the previous day and was unable to return to the ice after Game 2's pregame warm-up.[53]

"He deserves so much credit for what he did tonight, coming to the rink and going out there for a warm-up," said Julien after the game. "Certainly he did the best he could to even try. To be honest with you, it wasn't even close."

And neither was the game. Although Bergeron scored the B's first playoff goal of 2011 when he beat Price at 7:38 of the second, Yannick Weber scored the clincher.[54]

The Bruins were now down 0-2, with the next two games taking place in a building that had traditionally been a house of horrors.[55]

ABOVE: Shane Hnidy tried to give the Bruins a lift by taking on Canadien James Wisniewski.
RIGHT: Tim Thomas was in disbelief in Game 2 when Mathieu Darche put Montreal up by a score of 2-0.

53 Despite nausea, fatigue, and the fact he dropped approximately 10 pounds in 72 hours, Chara courageously attempted to play in Game 2 and skated in warm-ups. During the drills, he was dizzy and after the short 15-minute warm-up period concluded, Chara felt as if he just ran a marathon.

54 Following the Game 2 loss, Julien and Recchi provided some motivational words in the B's dressing room. "We are a good team and we are still capable of winning this series," Julien calmly told his charges. "We lost those two games because of our own doing. We just need to find our game and find that confidence. If we take care of Game 3, we'll get some momentum back and take off from there." Recchi then added, "Boys, when I was with Carolina we were down 0-2 and we went to Montreal and won the next two. We fought back to win that series and went on to win the Cup. It's doable, we just have to play our game and believe."

55 Julien made a key defensive adjustment heading into Game 3 that would pay huge dividends for the rest of the postseason. He decided to pair Chara and Seidenberg—his top two defensemen—together. It was important to slow down the swift Montreal attack and Julien felt the Chara-Seidenberg pair could do that since both were capable of logging big minutes (they each averaged north of 27 minutes per game in the playoffs). Very similar off the ice in terms of the pride they take in their fitness, their diet, and how they conduct themselves, the pair grew more and more comfortable on the ice as the postseason progressed, forming a dominant shutdown duo.

GAME 3 APRIL 18, 2011

BOSTON 4 MONTREAL 2

The scene shifted to Montreal's Bell Centre, where extra security precautions were taken to ensure the safety of the club in the light of the Pacioretty incident. But on the ice, the B's faced a really dire predicament as they came into the game 0-26 when down 0-2 in a playoff series.[56]

"We haven't won there this year," said Lucic pregame. "We have been a really good road team this year, but we're definitely the underdogs going into the rest of the series."

The underdogs took the third game however, as Krejci, Horton, and Peverley all beat Price and Kelly added an empty netter.

---

56 Bergeron believes the team leaned on experience gained from losing to Philadelphia the previous season. "We definitely learned from that series. It taught us you are never out of it until you lose that fourth game. There was no panic. We were still confident that if we played our game, we would be fine and come back and win the series."

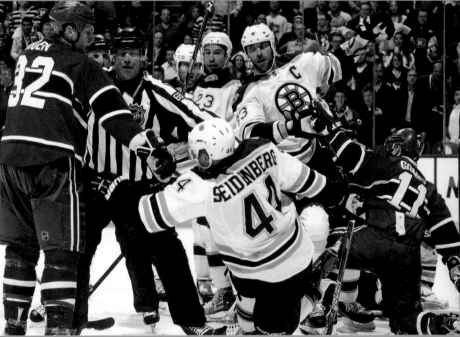

FAR LEFT: David Krejci, who scored Boston's first goal of Game 3, jumped to allow a shot through on Carey Price as Montreal's P.K. Subban looked on. CENTER: Mark Recchi approached a celebrating Rich Peverley after the game-winning goal in Game 3. ABOVE TOP: Montreal goaltender Carey Price couldn't cover the entire net as he yielded three goals before a Chris Kelly empty netter sealed the win for Boston. ABOVE MIDDLE: Daniel Paille was first in line to congratulate Tim Thomas on the Game 3 victory. ABOVE BOTTOM: *Left to right*: Travis Moen, Chris Kelly, Zdeno Chara, and Dennis Seidenberg, *front*, embodied the hard-fought series.

Lake Placid

By Tim Thomas

When the team returned to Lake Placid and the home rink of the 1980 "Miracle on Ice" Team USA and I first saw the American locker room, I immediately noticed how plain and pretty simple the room was. After just a few seconds, in my head, the wheels were turning recreating what happened those couple of weeks during the Lake Placid Olympics.

I was five years old at that time, and I already had some inkling that I wanted to be a goalie, but Jim Craig sealed the deal. I became a goalie, and my personal goal from age five until really probably age 20 was to play in the Olympics like Jim Craig. Not that I didn't want to play in the NHL; I'm from Flint, Michigan and we had a local IHL team, but there wasn't a lot of hockey on TV back in those days. Hockey Night in Canada was on once a week on a feed from above the border, and a grainy feed at that. So, I guess it wasn't unusual for an American hockey player from Michigan, but I remember from my early years the goal was the Olympics.

I attained that goal when I was chosen to represent the United States at the 2010 Vancouver games. It was everything I hoped it would be, and it was just an amazing atmosphere on the whole, but winning the silver reinforced what I already knew about 1980. What Herb Brooks, Craig, and his teammates accomplished was a huge moment for hockey in the United States and also for the USA as a country. In 1980 we were coming out of the "stagflation" of the '70s; we were coming out of the Cold War against Russia. The Russian team was supposed to be unbeatable, and a team of college kids was able to put it together and basically have a miracle tournament. So that, really, is on a whole different, higher level. The Miracle on Ice was a totally different beast.

As for the trip to Lake Placid and its effect on our team as we attempted to come back against Montreal, I can't be certain. But I do know that the break from being in a city like Montreal and a trip to the cozy town like Lake Placid simply helped us focus on hockey. And maybe, after practicing there between Game 3 and 4, just a little bit of the 1980 Miracle rubbed off on us, too.

OLYMPIC CENTER

Welcome to the site of the sports event of the century
USA 4   USSR 3
"MIRACLE ON ICE"   February 22, 1980

GAME 4 APRIL 21, 2011

BOSTON 5 MONTREAL 4 ot

Perhaps looking for a minor "Miracle," and certainly with a mind toward safety and privacy, the B's shifted their base of operations to Lake Placid, New York between the third and fourth games of the Eastern Conference quarterfinals.[57]

Thomas, among others, marveled at being able to visit the home rink of the 1980 gold medal-winning Team USA before they returned to the Bell Centre and Game 4.

The trip didn't pay immediate dividends—the club was down 3–1 halfway through the contest—and Head Coach Julien had to use his timeout 7:47 into the middle stanza to calm his club.[58] But goals by Ference (who was later fined for his goal celebration, an "unintentional bird")[59] and Bergeron tied the game. Montreal defenseman P.K. Subban scored a power play goal to put the Habs on top early in the third, but Kelly scored with 6:18 left in regulation to set up a Michael Ryder overtime goal at 1:59 of the extra session.

"You need your players to step up at this time of year," Julien said. "A lot of times there is a different guy stepping up and tonight it was Michael."

57   In a process akin to selecting the host city for a future Olympics, the Bruins chose Lake Placid, New York over "finalists" Mont Tremblant, Quebec and Burlington, Vermont as the location where they would spend their two off days in between Games 3 and 4. With the elevated tension and animosity between the two teams (and the two cities), management felt it would be best to go somewhere more relaxed and secluded so the team could focus on hockey and the task at hand, as opposed to the Montreal controversy. Head Athletic Trainer Don Del Negro—who spends his summers in Lake Placid—was instrumental in organizing the trip and used his connections to arrange all the lodging and dining logistics.

58   Julien was extremely positive during this timeout. He offered words of encouragement to the players, mentioned how the team was playing well, talked about believing in each other, and working on getting that next goal.

59   Ference regretfully admits that while his gloves were, in fact, brand new and rather stiff (his original alibi), his gesture was an "intentional bird" after all. The combination of being on the receiving end of a hard check earlier in the period, coupled with two vocal Habs fans seated right above the Bruins tunnel and a "caught-up-in-the-excitement" lapse of judgment caused the inappropriate reaction.

OPPOSITE: The Bruins vaulted off their bench to celebrate following the Michael Ryder, *top left*, overtime goal that evened their series at two games apiece.
TOP RIGHT: Patrice Bergeron's second period goal and assist in game four was crucial in evening the series against Montreal and goalie Carey Price.

GAME 5 APRIL 23, 2011

MONTREAL 1 BOSTON 2 2OT

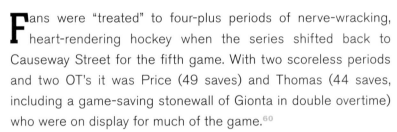

Fans were "treated" to four-plus periods of nerve-wracking, heart-rendering hockey when the series shifted back to Causeway Street for the fifth game. With two scoreless periods and two OT's it was Price (49 saves) and Thomas (44 saves, including a game-saving stonewall of Gionta in double overtime) who were on display for much of the game.[60]

But it was a save by Ryder that kept the game scoreless and sent his name trending worldwide.

When asked how he ended up in a classic goaltender pose in the Bruins crease, Ryder said he didn't know. "It was something like a two-on-one, three-on-one, and our 'D' went over and they just made a pass in front. I knew Timmy was out of position and I tried blocking any way I could, and ended up getting the glove on it."[61]

Marchand and Montreal's Jeff Halpern swapped goals in the third, but Horton's goal at 9:03 of the second OT gave Boston its first lead of the series.

---

60 Thomas had three spectacular saves this season that stood well above the rest: his improbable glove save on Toronto's Francois Beauchemin in OT on December 4 in Toronto, "The Save" (his diving stick save robbing Steve Downie on the doorstep in Game 5 against Tampa in the Eastern Conference Finals), and his two-on-one, post-to-post save on Brian Gionta in Game 5 against Montreal in OT. In Thomas' opinion, while the save on Downie probably looked prettier for the cameras, it was the save on Gionta that was more important and more timely. If he hadn't made that stop, the game would've been over and the Bruins would've headed back to Montreal facing elimination, down three games to two.

61 Ryder actually plays goalie for his ball hockey team back in Newfoundland during the summers. Even so, this was still an unorthodox save, as he stopped the puck with his right hand, which is his blocker hand and not his glove hand.

TOP LEFT: Nathan Horton and Tim Thomas celebrated Boston's first lead of the series. TOP RIGHT: Michael Ryder channeled his ball-hockey roots as a goalie to make a save; *left to right*: Andrei Kostitsyn, Ryder, Dennis Seidenberg, Tomas Plekanec, Tim Thomas. BOTTOM LEFT: Nathan Horton ended the 12th longest game in Bruins history after 89:03 of play. BOTTOM RIGHT: Andrew Ference was the first teammate to mob Horton after the double overtime score.

GAME 6 APRIL 26, 2011

BOSTON 1 MONTREAL 2

The B's felt like they let a major opportunity fall away when they dropped Game 6.

"They scored two goals five-on-three," explained Julien of the penalty marred playoff game. "Five-on-four they weren't a threat and neither were we. Five-on-five I thought we were obviously the team that held most of the control of the game. It's one of those games where we tried, we worked hard, we had our chances, and we weren't able to bury them."

Seidenberg buried the B's only goal seconds into the second period, but Cammalleri and Gionta each scored their third goals of the series,[62] while Price made 31 saves to pace the Habs.

---

62   Gionta had a goal disallowed earlier in the game at 3:27 of the first period after a quick
      whistle blew the play dead, despite the fact the puck was still loose in Thomas' crease.
      This tough call prompted Montreal fans to litter the Bell Centre ice with promotional
      towels that were handed out just minutes earlier.

TOP LEFT: Tim Thomas stretched to make a save as, *left to right*, Zdeno Chara, Scott Gomez, and Dennis Seidenberg looked on. BOTTOM LEFT: Brad Marchand and a Canadien battled for space in the tight fought game. TOP RIGHT: Dennis Seidenberg skated across the Canadiens logo at center ice. BOTTOM RIGHT: Seidenberg checked Scott Gomez over Tim Thomas in the crease.

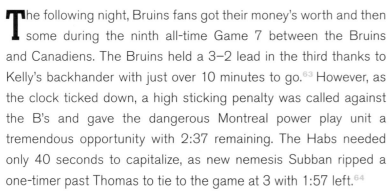

GAME 7 APRIL 27, 2011

MONTREAL 3 BOSTON 4 OT

The following night, Bruins fans got their money's worth and then some during the ninth all-time Game 7 between the Bruins and Canadiens. The Bruins held a 3–2 lead in the third thanks to Kelly's backhander with just over 10 minutes to go.[63] However, as the clock ticked down, a high sticking penalty was called against the B's and gave the dangerous Montreal power play unit a tremendous opportunity with 2:37 remaining. The Habs needed only 40 seconds to capitalize, as new nemesis Subban ripped a one-timer past Thomas to tie to the game at 3 with 1:57 left.[64]

However, in overtime, Horton heard a "Woo" 5:43 into the extra session and sent the Bruins on to the Eastern Conference Semis.

"I don't remember too much. I remember Looch coming up with the puck and I just tried to get open, and I tried putting the puck toward the net. Luckily it got deflected off someone and it went straight in. That's all I remember," Horton said.

Nathan might not remember the moment, but everyone rooting for the Black & Gold—who improved to 1-26 when down 0-2 in a seven game series—will certainly recall Horton's goal for a long, long time.

---

63   The Kelly-Peverley-Ryder line was superb in this first round, combining for six goals and eight assists in the seven games.

64   While most of the 17,565 in attendance at the TD Garden were deflated heading into OT, the Bruins remained poised and confident. Addressing the team at the third intermission, Julien told the players that they needed to be aggressive to start the overtime period and play to win. "We worked our way back into this series. This series belongs to us," he said. "No regrets, let's go out there and get it."

TOP LEFT: Mark Recchi and Brad Marchand celebrated a Boston goal. TOP MIDDLE: Recchi gave the Bruins a 2–0 lead just 5:33 into Game 7. BOTTOM MIDDLE: The Bruins celebrated their first Game 7 win since 1994. ABOVE: Milan Lucic made the pass to Nathan Horton, who scored his second overtime goal of the series, *bottom*, and the celebration commenced, *top*.

CHAPTER SIX

PATIENCE PAYS OFF

EASTERN CONFERENCE
SEMIFINAL

To say that the Bruins players were sick of hearing about their 2010 fold versus the Flyers would be an understatement, but during a brisk afternoon press conference between his club's victory over Montreal in Round 1 and the B's leaving for Philadelphia for Round 2, Boston Bruins General Manager Peter Chiarelli was asked if the Black & Gold relished a rematch with the Flyers.

"I do, of course. I think the players do," Chiarelli said. "It's fitting that we're playing them."[65]

But getting by the Flyers would be another issue entirely.

"Well they're bigger, first and foremost," Chiarelli said when asked to compare and contrast Philadelphia and Montreal. "I think that's a huge difference.

"They're like us to a certain degree. They've got skill players, they've got some heavy players and obviously there's more similarities between us and them than there are between us and Montreal."[66]

Chiarelli also talked about differences between his current Bruins team and the team that let a 3-0 series lead slip away the previous spring.

"I believe in Game 7 of last year, there were nine players in that game that are on our roster now," Chiarelli said. "So, there's been more than half the team that's turned over, but definitely the core players also lived through that. It's been a consistent theme this year."

---

65 At the beginning of the season, Coach Julien had instructed his players to keep the Philadelphia series from last year in the back of their minds and take lessons from it, but not dwell on it. During the 2011 playoff series with Philadelphia, he never once brought it up as a motivational tool. He believed that deep down, everyone knew what this series meant. It didn't need to be said.

66 Thomas had circled two regular season dates with the Flyers as "measuring stick" games for him personally early in the year. He knew the Flyers were one of the best teams in the league and that their size, speed, and skill would be a good test for him and his repaired hip. In the first meeting, he made 41 saves in a 3–0 shutout on the road and followed that up with a strong 33-save performance in a 2–1 OT loss.

OPPOSITE: Tim Thomas gave his trademark post-win salute in net. ABOVE: Peter Chiarelli looked forward to the rematch with the Flyers in the conference semifinal series.

GAME 1 APRIL 30, 2011

BOSTON 7 PHILADELPHIA 3

One of the major obstacles the team that dropped four straight games to Philadelphia was the absence of David Krejci, who was injured for the final four games of the 2010 playoffs versus Philly. Krejci seemed destined to make a big impact on the 2011 playoffs, but after the Montreal series had only one goal and his line with Lucic and Horton had only six points combined.[67]

Krejci made an immediate impact on the second round, and his two goals and two assists in the first game of the Eastern Conference semifinals were just the tip of an iceberg that hit up Philly for seven goals—the club's best offensive output in a playoff game since 1988—as Marchand (2 goals, 1 assist) and Bergeron (3 assists) each added three point games.[68]

---

67 In the days leading up to the series opener, Julien emphasized building on what they accomplished in the previous series against Montreal and the importance of winning that first game to put the Flyers on their heels.

68 Game 1 was played Saturday afternoon in Philadelphia, leaving the players with a rare free night during the playoffs. Showing once again how close the group had become, the players organized a team UFC Watch Party at their hotel to watch the big ultimate fighting event.

TOP LEFT: David Krejci had the team's first four-point playoff game since 2009 in Game 1 versus the Flyers. MIDDLE: Zdeno Chara conferred with Patrice Bergeron during the game. TOP RIGHT: The line of, *left to right*, Brad Marchand, Patrice Bergeron, and Mark Recchi combined for seven points in the Game 1 victory. MIDDLE RIGHT: Chris Kelly, Adam McQuaid, and Dennis Seidenberg congratulated Tim Thomas following the win. BOTTOM RIGHT: David Krejci scored three of the four game-winning goals of the series, becoming one of just three Bruins to accomplish that feat.

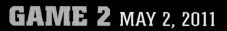

GAME 2 MAY 2, 2011

BOSTON 3 PHILADELPHIA 2 OT

Another Hockey East alumnus haunted the B's early in the second game of the Eastern Conference semis as former UNH standout James Van Riemsdyk scored two goals in the first period, but Kelly and Marchand both scored for Boston in the opening stanza and the game remained 2–2 until Krejci scored his third goal of the series at 14:00 of OT.

Thomas was again spectacular, and made 46 straight saves, including 22 stops in the third period, to get the game to overtime and finished the contest with 52 saves on 54 Flyers shots (the third

most shots against for Boston in their playoff history and the highest total since 1947).[69] Van Riemsdyk had a tremendous game in the losing effort, finishing with the two goals, eight shots, and a hefty 28:18 of ice time.

---

69   Thomas said he felt unbeatable from the second period on and felt more confident in this contest than any other in the 2011 postseason.

OPPOSITE: In the closest game of the series, Brian Boucher made a stop on David Krejci, *top left*, Patrice Bergeron battled Ville Leino in the faceoff circle, *top right*, and Tim Thomas made one of his 52 saves while Chris Kelly looked on, *bottom*. ABOVE: Johnny Boychuk battled Ville Leino for the puck along the boards.

GAME 3 MAY 4, 2011

PHILADELPHIA 1 BOSTON 5

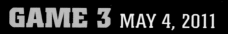

It was an offensive explosion for the Bruins, who took it to the Flyers with the fastest opening two goals in team playoff history when Chara scored at the 30 second mark of the first and Krejci added a tally at 1:03.

Both men also had three-point evenings, as Horton earned a Gordie Howe hat trick with a goal, a fight, and an assist, Boston's first playoff Howe-trick since April 20, 1988.[70]

70 It was déjà vu all over again as Boston had the chance to sweep the Flyers after taking a commanding 3-0 series lead in the Eastern Conference semis. It didn't need to be said in the dressing room, but everyone understood. "There was no way we were going to let them back in the series," Julien said. "We were determined to end the series right there and then."

OPPOSITE: A table of rally towels awaited fans shortly before the turnstiles opened for Game 3. MIDDLE: David Krejci and linemate Nathan Horton combined for two of the Bruins' five goals in Game 3. TOP RIGHT: Horton's Gordie Howe hat trick included a fight with the Flyers' Sean O'Donnell. MIDDLE RIGHT: Zdeno Chara celebrated one of his two goals of the game with Brad Marchand. BOTTOM RIGHT: Tim Thomas made one of his 37 saves in the 5–1 win.

GAME 4 MAY 6, 2011

PHILADELPHIA 1 BOSTON 5

It started out close. Thanks to assists from Horton and Krejci (who ended the series with a 4-5-9 line) Lucic opened the scoring for Boston in the first and Philadelphia's Kris Versteeg added his own in the second, but the B's broke out in the third.

Boychuk beat Philly backup Sergei Bobrovsky and Lucic scored his second of the game and of the playoffs to set up Marchand and Paille's empty net coup de grace.

"We were up three-nothing," Boychuk said. "We wanted to close it off and we did.

"We had everybody going tonight."

Unfortunately, not everyone was going by the end of the game as a third-period hit by Philadelphia's Claude Giroux left Bergeron with a slight concussion and put his availability for Round 3 in question. The fact that Round 3 would not begin for eight days would certainly work to Bergeron's advantage, but its effect on the team as a whole would remain to be seen.[71]

71 This situation was eerily similar to the Bruins-Hurricanes series in the '09 playoffs, when the B's swept an opponent only to have eight days off in between games. After the Bruins were bounced by Carolina in '09, many players had mentioned how the long layoff took away the momentum they had built and was detrimental to the overall focus of the team. In '09, some players saw the time off as an opportunity to relax and spend time doing leisurely activities, such as golf. Not this year. Recchi actually addressed this in a team meeting in Wilmington. Drawing on experience from that Carolina series, Recchi made the entire roster pledge to one another that their focus would remain on hockey during the layoff and there would be no golf until the season was over.

TOP LEFT: A Bruins fan felt confident that there would be no Flyers comeback like last postseason. TOP MIDDLE: Milan Lucic beat Flyers goaltender Sergei Bobrovsky with one of his two goals in the deciding Game 4. BOTTOM MIDDLE: The Bruins saluted their fans at game's end as Boston advanced to the conference final for the first time since 1992. TOP RIGHT: David Krejci celebrated Lucic's opening score in the first period. BOTTOM RIGHT: Two Bruins fans made their allegiance clear.

Believe

During the Stanley Cup playoffs, the word *Believe*, along with a stenciled Bruins logo, started to appear all over town.

The *Believe* campaign was led by The Bear, the B's famous surly enforcer from the award-winning *Bruins Hockey Rules* advertising campaign, and the rallying cry could be found "etched" into city streets with power washers and "painted" with spray snow all over town, on everything from storefront windows to fire trucks.

Famous Boston landmarks even got into the act, as the George Washington and *Make Way for Ducklings* statues in the Public Garden and the Paul Revere statue in the North End were all adorned with personalized Bruins sweaters. As the calendar turned to June, there wasn't a soul left in the region that had not caught Bruins fever.

EASTERN CONFERENCE
FINAL

History, hatred, or redemption weren't exactly watchwords while the Bruins prepared for their matchup with the Tampa Bay Lightning.

Thanks to the shared collegiate hockey heritage of the Bolts' Martin St. Louis and the B's Thomas (both men played together for four seasons at the University of Vermont), as well as the feel-good storyline that pitted the Lightning's aged and unconventional goalie Dwayne Roloson versus the "modified butterfly" of Boston's own veteran goalie—it was almost a love-in.

"When I wasn't in the NHL, I was looking at Dwayne Roloson," said Thomas pre-series. "He made it to the NHL and I don't know how long it took him after he got out of college, but he really had to work his way up before he got those No. 1 jobs.

"I saw that he was doing it and it's something that can give you hope."

In the end, however, it was Thomas who would dash the hopes of hockey fans in Tampa Bay.

GAME 1 MAY 14, 2011
TAMPA BAY 5 BOSTON 1

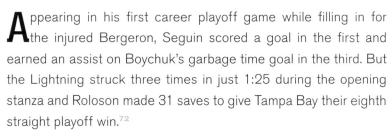

Appearing in his first career playoff game while filling in for the injured Bergeron, Seguin scored a goal in the first and earned an assist on Boychuk's garbage time goal in the third. But the Lightning struck three times in just 1:25 during the opening stanza and Roloson made 31 saves to give Tampa Bay their eighth straight playoff win.[72]

The B's did not convert on four man-advantage opportunities and stood 2/41 on the power play during the playoffs.[73]

---

72 His trademark glass of red wine in hand after Game 1, Recchi privately remarked, "Losing this game like that was the best thing to happen. We needed a wake-up call." He felt the team wasn't sharp heading into the contest and that the loss would recalibrate their focus and that they'd come back strong in Game 2.

73 On Monday, May 16 (the practice before Game 2), the Bruins power play was on the ice before the full session began. The B's started out with a 5-on-0 drill (no penalty killers on the ice) and Seguin, who was out with the power play unit for the first time in the playoffs, found himself with the first shot opportunity of the practice. His shot accidentally struck Lucic squarely on the big toe, the force cracking and crushing the toe to the point that it was compressed. Seguin immediately apologized (injuring anyone besides the goalie in a 5-on-0 drill is not very common) and the two shared a laugh about Seguin's "friendly fire" later. "You don't realize how much push you get off your big toe when you skate," Lucic said. "Even putting a shoe on was tough after that. I couldn't walk normally without a limp for two weeks."

TOP LEFT: Tyler Seguin scored his first career playoff goal versus Tampa Bay's Dwayne Roloson. BOTTOM LEFT: The Lightning congratulated their goaltender after drawing the series' first blood.
ABOVE: Tampa's Simon Gagne, who had broken the hearts of Bruins fans as a Flyer in 2010, celebrated a goal with Vincent Lecavalier as Tim Thomas and Andrew Ference reacted.

GAME 2 MAY 17, 2011

TAMPA BAY 5 BOSTON 6

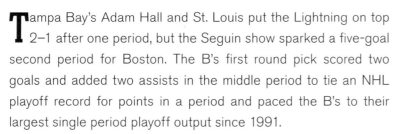

Tampa Bay's Adam Hall and St. Louis put the Lightning on top 2–1 after one period, but the Seguin show sparked a five-goal second period for Boston. The B's first round pick scored two goals and added two assists in the middle period to tie an NHL playoff record for points in a period and paced the B's to their largest single period playoff output since 1991.

"I try to take everything in and learn as much as I can, but it's hard sitting there and not being able to help the boys," Seguin said. "I wanted to take advantage of every opportunity I got."[74]

---

74   When the playoffs started, Shawn Thornton had noticed that Seguin's practice habits were basically the same as they were in the regular season. Not that the habits were bad, but Thornton knew from experience that in the postseason, practice intensity and preparation needs to be elevated so he pulled the rookie aside. "These practices are your games until you get in. If we are going to win it, you are going to play at some point and we are going to need you," he said. "Injuries happen, suspensions happen. You are going to have to be ready for when you come in. You need to work your ass off and make sure you are on top of your game when we do finally need you."

OPPOSITE: Tyler Seguin saluted the crowd as the game's First Star after matching a league record with a four-point second period. ABOVE: Nathan Horton evened the score at 1–1 with a first-period power play score. BOTTOM LEFT: Seguin's second goal of the period left Dwayne Roloson flailing in his crease. BOTTOM MIDDLE: Of the 11 goals scored in Game 2, none was more important than Michael Ryder's at 19:41 of the second period, which proved to be the game-winner. BOTTOM RIGHT: Tampa's Steven Stamkos could only watch as David Krejci gave the Bruins a 3-2 lead in the game.

GAME 3 MAY 19, 2011

BOSTON 2 TAMPA BAY 0

Bergeron rejoined the lineup as Seguin remained on the roster and Thornton sat out, but it was Thomas (31 saves, shutout) and Krejci (fourth game-winner of the playoffs to tie a Bruins record) who set the tone as Boston took a 2-1 lead in the series.[75]

"Obviously, you work your whole life to be in this situation, you don't want to watch games once you get here, but in the big picture you look at it and I'm the right choice at this point," Thornton later said.

75   Heading into the series with Tampa, the Bruins staff expected a chess match with the well-coached and offensively gifted Bolts. When preparing his team for this series, Julien emphasized the importance of patience and getting pucks in behind the Tampa defensemen in order to crack Tampa's vaunted 1-3-1 system. Limiting turnovers in the neutral zone was also imperative, as the Lightning were quick to generate scoring chances after forcing turnovers in the middle of the ice.

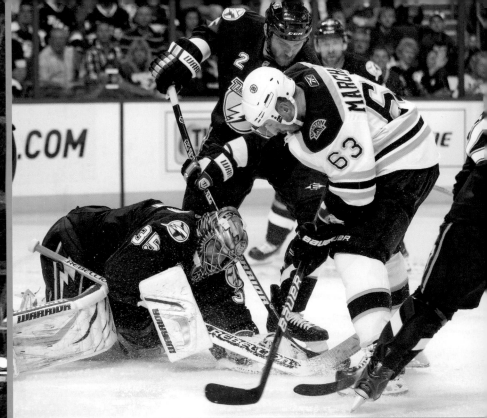

OPPOSITE TOP: David Krejci gets by Tampa's Steve Downie en route to scoring the game-winning goal, his fourth of the postseason which tied a club playoff record. OPPOSITE BOTTOM AND MIDDLE: Tim Thomas made 31 saves for his first shutout of the postseason. ABOVE TOP: Brad Marchand battles for net-front real estate against a pair of Lightning players and goalie Dwayne Roloson. ABOVE BOTTOM: Tyler Seguin celebrated the insurance goal as Tampa's Marc-Andre Bergeron and Roloson could only watch.

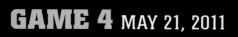

GAME 4 MAY 21, 2011

BOSTON 3 TAMPA BAY 5

Bergeron was back with a vengeance as he scored two unassisted goals (one shorthanded) as the B's chased Roloson after 18 minutes of play and took a three-goal cushion to the first intermission. But the Lightning's Teddy Purcell scored two of his own as Tampa Bay put five unanswered tallies on the board in the second and the third periods to send the series back to Boston tied, 2-2.[76]

[76] This game was a prime example of the Bruins not adhering to the "Full 60 Minutes" mentality. The first period was one of the team's best periods of the playoffs, but that was followed by two of the team's worst. Instead of taking a commanding 3-1 lead heading back home for Game 5, Tampa knotted the series at 2 and took back the momentum.

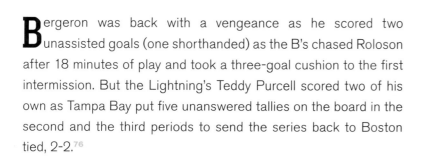

OPPOSITE: Tampa's Teddy Purcell, *top*, scored twice in a 1:03 span of the second to pull the Lightning to within 3-2, and Simon Gagne, *bottom*, netted the game-winner in the third despite the efforts of, *left to right*, Tomas Kaberle, Tim Thomas, and Dennis Seidenberg. ABOVE: *Left to right*: Patrice Bergeron, Johnny Boychuk, and Zdeno Chara celebrated Bergeron's shorthanded goal, which gave the Bruins a 3-0 first period lead.

GAME 5 MAY 23, 2011

TAMPA BAY 1 BOSTON 3

Thomas added to his highlight reel with a paddle save that robbed Tampa Bay's Steve Downie and kept the B's in command of a tight one-goal game. Goalie Mike Smith, who relieved Roloson in Game 4, was in for the Lightning, but wasn't able to keep Horton and Marchand at bay[77] and Peverley iced the game with an empty netter.

"Against this goaltender, you need more," said Lightning Head Coach Guy Boucher of Thomas' heroics. "You need miracles. Thomas is making miracles. We have to come up with miracles."

---

77   The Recchi-Bergeron-Marchand line was probably the most consistent line throughout the playoffs from start to finish. On this goal, Marchand kept the puck in the Tampa zone after a failed clearing attempt and after seeing Bergeron control the puck in the far corner, drove the net hard. Bergeron found the streaking Marchand with a perfect tape-to-tape pass and the rookie buried it for his sixth of the postseason.

OPPOSITE: Rich Peverley capped the victory with an empty net goal, as the Bruins closed to within one win of their first Stanley Cup Final appearance since 1990.
ABOVE: Tim Thomas' astounding stick save on Tampa's Steve Downie was best described by Lightning Coach Guy Boucher as "making miracles."

GAME 6 MAY 25, 2011

BOSTON 4 TAMPA BAY 5

Despite a playoff hat trick for Krejci (the Bruins first since Neely netted three back in 1991), Roloson improved to 7-0 in elimination games. Tampa Bay converted on three of four power play opportunities, while the B's were held to 20 shots for the second straight contest.[78]

---

78 After the Bruins lost Game 6 (which was an 8 p.m. start on Wednesday night), the coaching staff decided it would be best to stay overnight in Tampa and fly out in the morning. Normal procedure during the regular season would be to fly home immediately after the game, but Julien felt it would be best for the players to get their rest and use Thursday as a travel day with no practice, as opposed to getting home around 3 a.m. Thursday morning and skating later in the day.

TOP LEFT: Brad Marchand and Tyler Seguin participated in the traditional soccer warm-up prior to each game. ABOVE: *Left to right*: Johnny Boychuk, Nathan Horton, and Daniel Paille celebrated David Krejci's first of three goals of Game 6. INSET: Tampa's Steven Stamkos and Martin St. Louis combined for three goals, including the game-winner, to stave off elimination in Game 6.

GAME 7 MAY 27, 2011

TAMPA BAY 0 BOSTON 1

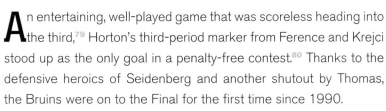

An entertaining, well-played game that was scoreless heading into the third,[79] Horton's third-period marker from Ference and Krejci stood up as the only goal in a penalty-free contest.[80] Thanks to the defensive heroics of Seidenberg and another shutout by Thomas, the Bruins were on to the Final for the first time since 1990.

"Well, he certainly has played like a big-game player," said Julien of Horton's series clincher. "Overtime goals, game-winning goals, I thought it was fitting, not just for him, but for our team."

Each and every Bruin had contributed in this series in one way or another.[81] From Seguin to the defensive heroics of Seidenberg and Chara, to the penalty killers who held the dangerous Tampa power play in check, this series was a total team effort.

Thanks to a little pre-planning by Chara, Recchi, and Bergeron, the Eastern Conference champions knew what they wanted to do with the Prince of Wales Trophy as it was presented to the captain.[82] The trophy, thought to be a source of bad karma for any team that raised or celebrated with the hardware, looked to have a superstition-fueled force field around it as the upbeat, but very composed, Bruins gathered in a three-foot arc around the trophy for a team picture, refusing to come in contact with it.

No matter, B's fans, ecstatic at the club's first Final appearance since 1990 did the celebrating for the Black & Gold as Causeway Street became party central. The TD Garden faithful filed into the West End and seemingly stayed downtown until the Bruins boarded buses for Logan Airport on Monday morning. A very impressive crowd of about 2,000 gathered to sendoff the B's in style to Vancouver.

"This is a great position to be in for a hockey player," said Horton before the team departed. "It keeps getting harder and harder to describe into words, but so far it's been amazing and I'm sure it's just going to keep getting better."

ABOVE TOP: Coach Julien congratulated his team on their conference title while reminding them of the work still to be done. MIDDLE TOP: This scramble in front of the Boston net illustrated the determination of both teams not to be eliminated. MIDDLE: Tim Thomas and his college teammate, Tampa's Martin St. Louis, shared a moment during the handshake line following the game. RIGHT: Captain Zdeno Chara, here checking former Bruin Nate Thompson along the boards, was his usual dominating presence in the series-clinching Game 7. BOTTOM: Nathan Horton scored his second straight Game 7 winner with the game's only tally at 12:27 of the third period.

79 During the second intermission, confidence was high inside the Bruins dressing room. Although they had yet to score, the team was controlling play and had been skating extremely well: they were getting pucks in behind the Tampa defense, forechecking, and limiting turnovers. Rather than try and do anything different to beat Roloson—who was outstanding from start to finish—Julien preached a message of "maintaining" what they had been doing in the first two periods. "Be patient, stick with it. Eventually it will come," he told the team during his intermission speech. Those words were heeded, as that "patience" is exactly what led to Horton's game-winner.

80 Ference's patience paid off in the game-winner. As he carried the puck out of his own end with Simon Gagne the lone Tampa forechecker in the neutral zone, the veteran defenseman had a few options: he could safely pass "D-to-D" to Boychuk on his right or dump the puck in deep in the Tampa zone. Instead, he took an extra stride and brought the puck a little deeper into the neutral zone. This little hesitation drew in Tampa's Purcell and opened a narrow passing lane for Ference to hit Krejci. The pass was perfect. Krejci took the feed, skated with speed down the left side, and slipped a beautiful pass under the stick of Tampa defenseman Eric Brewer. Horton was there on the doorstep and deflected it past Roloson for the series clincher.

81 And not just on the ice. Sitting in a hotel room after the Game 6 loss, scratches Shawn Thornton and Shane Hnidy were thinking about ways they could help the team even though they weren't in the lineup. They devised a plan that would hopefully help inspire their teammates by showing them just how close they were to achieving something very, very special. They asked the Bruins equipment staff of Keith Robinson, Beets Johnson, and Matt Falconer to get framed pictures that featured  images of Bruins greats like Bobby Orr, Derek Sanderson, and John Bucyk celebrating their Stanley Cup victories and hang them in the Bruins locker room at the TD Garden. Assisted by TD Garden sports memorabilia guru Bob Rutko, the equipment staff found these pictures and hung the photos in the locker room the afternoon of Game 7. Thornton also coordinated with Recchi and Assistant Coach Doug Jarvis to bring in their Stanley Cup rings and display them in the locker room, to again show their teammates what they were on the verge of attaining.

82 Chara had mentioned to Recchi and Bergeron before Game 7 that he wanted to do a team picture with the trophy after they won, as he didn't think it was appropriate for him to pose on his own. When he skated toward the trophy, he would wave the team in and Recchi and Bergeron were responsible for making sure the rest of the team followed. The response was tremendous. "It was a nice gesture I thought," said Chara, who was told after the fact a team picture with the Prince of Wales Trophy had never been done before. "It was a real special moment to have the whole team there and it turned out to be a great picture."

CHAPTER SEVEN

WHATEVER IT TAKES⁸³

STANLEY CUP
FINAL

As many Bruins fans can tell you, 39 years is a long time. But those same fans will also tell you that the 15 days that encapsulated the 2011 Stanley Cup Final between the Vancouver Canucks and the Boston Bruins were just as torturous as the previous 14,264, but were infinitely more entertaining and rewarding.

In Twitter parlance, #VanBos was seven games of top notch hockey action, sandwiched between on and off ice trash talk, fingers pointed and fingers bitten, inspirational returns and even more inspirational farewells. And, oh yeah, there was some tire pumping in there too. But given the history of disappointment since Johnny Bucyk last carried the Cup off the ice in 1972, the Black & Gold faithful could be excused if they were a little nervous going up against the Presidents' Trophy winners. After all, the Canucks were prohibitive favorites going into the series.[84]

However, as the Bruins packed their bags and headed west,[85] there was some bristling when they were questioned about the frenzied, overwhelming hockey atmosphere in Vancouver. Granted, in 2010 Vancouver had hosted one of the greatest Olympic Hockey Tournaments of all time, but the city had not yet seen its Canucks raise the Cup.

"I don't think it gets any crazier than Montreal," said Seidenberg, downplaying any effect the Canucks fans would have on his team's performance. "I'm sure everybody knows what to expect and is ready to handle it."

Given the comments that would follow later, it's also interesting to note Thomas' answer when he was asked about the upcoming goaltending matchup.

"It's not me versus Luongo," Thomas said. "I watched the last game he played there against San Jose and he looked real good.

"I know that I'm going to have to do a good job to give our team a chance."

83 Since the start of the playoffs, a whiteboard hung in the TD Garden equipment room that always had two items written on it: a to-do list that counted down the number of wins needed to win the Stanley Cup and the slogan "Whatever It Takes." This mentality was adopted by not just the players, but the entire team staff as well. From the "eye-in-the-sky" Doug Jarvis, to medical staffers Scott Waugh and Derek Repucci, to Video Analyst Jeremy Rogalski through Strength Coach John Whitesides, everyone was willing to do "whatever it took" to help the team succeed, regardless of whether or not it fell in their job description.

84 While few outside the Bruins dressing room were picking the Bruins, taking a look at the Bruins scouting reports of the Canucks and their individual players, it's no wonder the Bruins liked their chances heading into this series. The reports stated that the way to beat the Canucks and their high-powered offense was to dominate their skill players physically. Hit the Sedin twins, Alexandre Burrows, Ryan Kesler, etc. all over the ice and make them pay the price for coming near Thomas' crease. As the series went deeper, the reports said, the Canucks would eventually wear down as a result of the punishment they received in the corners and around the Bruins net. The Black & Gold loved this strategy, as there weren't many teams in the NHL better constructed to execute a game plan based upon physicality all over the ice than the 2011 Boston Bruins.

85 One interesting piece of equipment the Bruins carried with them on the road was a portable heat/air conditioner/dehumidifier unit that controlled the air quality and temperature inside the B's locker room. "We didn't want to leave the climate in our dressing room in the hands of the opposing team's building," said Head Equipment Manager Keith Robinson, noting that if any visiting team's building tried to sabotage the climate in the Bruins locker room, this unit would be able to combat it.

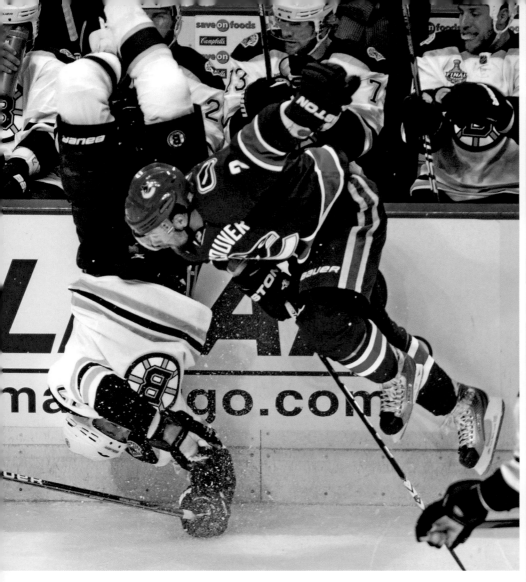

GAME 1 JUNE 1, 2011

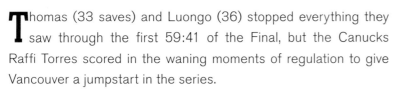

BOSTON 0 VANCOUVER 1

Thomas (33 saves) and Luongo (36) stopped everything they saw through the first 59:41 of the Final, but the Canucks Raffi Torres scored in the waning moments of regulation to give Vancouver a jumpstart in the series.

Vancouver's Alex Burrows turned up the heat in the Final when it appeared he bit Bergeron's finger during an altercation after the first period.

"Oh yeah, he did," confirmed Bergeron. "He cut me a little bit on my finger.

"I'm not gonna sit here and complain about it—I'll let the league do their job—but he sure did."

Beyond the mastication, Vancouver brought a very physical style to Rogers Arena, but the Canucks lost key defenseman Dan Hamhuis to injury after he landed a big hit on Lucic.[86]

---

86   Hamhuis upended Lucic along the boards by the benches on this hit, sending the burly Bruin winger head over skates. However, Hamhuis immediately went back to the medical room and ultimately would not return for the entire series. While originally listed as "day-to-day," it was later learned that he sustained three significant injuries on the one play: unspecified injuries to both his groin and lower abdomen and a sports hernia.

OPPOSITE: Vancouver's Dan Hamhuis got the better of Milan Lucic with this hit but injured himself on the play and was lost to the Canucks for the remainder of the series. ABOVE: The nasty tone of the series was set early as evidenced by, *left to right*, Vancouver's Alexandre Burrows' bite on Patrice Bergeron and Boston's dominance of Canucks captain Henrik Sedin.

TOP LEFT: *Left to right*: Johnny Boychuk, Brad Marchand, Mark Recchi, Patrice Bergeron, and Zdeno Chara stood at attention during the national anthems at the start of the Stanley Cup Final series. TOP RIGHT: Chris Kelly took a faceoff against the Canucks' Maxim Lapierre. BOTTOM LEFT: Dennis Seidenberg confronted Vancouver's Daniel Sedin.
BOTTOM RIGHT: Despite Zdeno Chara's net-front presence, Roberto Luongo stopped all 36 shots he faced for a 1-0 Canucks win in Game 1.

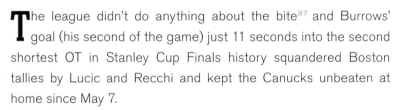

GAME 2 JUNE 4, 2011

BOSTON 2 VANCOUVER 3 OT

The league didn't do anything about the bite[87] and Burrows' goal (his second of the game) just 11 seconds into the second shortest OT in Stanley Cup Finals history squandered Boston tallies by Lucic and Recchi and kept the Canucks unbeaten at home since May 7.

Former Canadien turned Canuck Maxim Lapierre tried to get Bergeron to bite him when he taunted the B's center during a third-period dustup. Needless to say, Lapierre was unsuccessful.

The Bruins returned to Boston down 0-2, a situation that had previously seen only four teams come back to take the Cup.[88]

"We've been able to bounce back all playoffs," Thomas said. "But every time you do it, you have to put in the work to turn it around. It doesn't just happen so we're going to have to do what we need to do to get ready and to be ready to win Game 3."

---

87 Burrows did not receive a suspension—as the league couldn't find conclusive evidence that he intentionally bit Bergeron—and the Canucks went on to mock the situation in a segment aired on NBC during Game 2. Asked to introduce his linemates, Henrik Sedin responded "Hi, I'm Henrik Sedin, this is my brother Daniel, and on the other side, we have the vegetarian Alex Burrows."

88 There was frustration in the Bruins locker room after Game 2, but not panic. Julien reminded the players that coming back after being down 0-2 was not uncharted territory for this group. And in fact, they were actually in a better position in this series than they were in Round 1 against Montreal since they had the next two games at home. The Bruins turned their focus on Game 3, knowing that a win in that game would put them right back into the series and swing the momentum in their favor.

TOP LEFT: Zdeno Chara and Patrice Bergeron congratulated Mark Recchi after giving the Bruins a 2-1 lead midway through Game 2. ABOVE: Alexandre Burrows, *center*, celebrated his goal, which ended the second-shortest overtime in Final history, as Andrew Ference, Johnny Boychuk, and Tim Thomas contemplated returning to Boston down 0-2 in the series.

TOP LEFT: The visitors dressing room at Rogers Arena awaited its occupants on the afternoon of Game 2. TOP RIGHT: Brad Marchand and Patrice Bergeron created traffic in front of Roberto Luongo. BOTTOM LEFT: Tim Thomas upended Daniel Sedin on this chance, but Sedin would score the game-tying goal in the third period, which set up Burrows' heroics. BOTTOM MIDDLE: Vancouver native Milan Lucic celebrated his second-period goal, but the crowd wasn't celebrating with their hometown son. BOTTOM RIGHT: Adam McQuaid checked Chris Higgins during Game 2.

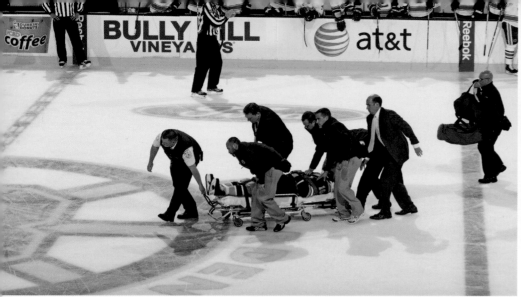

GAME 3 JUNE 6, 2011

VANCOUVER 1 BOSTON 8

The "Big Bad Bruins" were back on this night.[89]

The scoresheet from the third game of the Final reads like Tolstoy's *War and Peace*, but the Bruins and their fans needed only to see the first two infractions—a five-minute interference penalty and a game misconduct to Aaron Rome for a hit on Nathan Horton—to see red.

The rest of the game was colored Black & Gold as Thornton returned in Seguin's stead[90] and so did the Bruins swagger. Goals from Ference, Krejci, Marchand, Paille, Kelly, Ryder, and two goals from Recchi fueled the B's offensive explosion, but the B's reaction to the Burrows' bite and Lapierre's taunting gave a new edge to Boston's game.[91]

In the aftermath, neither Horton (concussion) nor Rome (suspension) would return to the series.[92]

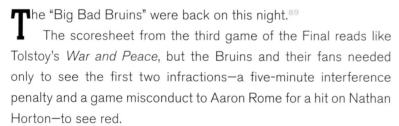

TOP LEFT: Nathan Horton was lost for the series following a first-period blindside hit, but the Bruins took their revenge on the scoresheet with an eight-goal outburst over the final two stanzas. BOTTOM LEFT: Adam McQuaid was upended by former Bruin Andrew Alberts. RIGHT: Brad Marchand's shorthanded goal had the rookie flying high with teammate Andrew Ference.

89 Before the teams hit the ice for Game 3, a fired-up Chara gathered his teammates in the locker room and gave his most intense talk of the playoffs. His message? Be physical. Be mean. And be *nasty*. "We need to play hard and push the physical play all the way to the limits," said the captain, who, in his own words "went nuts" during this talk. "Go after them. Really physical tonight boys. Everybody's physical, take it to them!" They listened. The B's outhit the Canucks 40-31 and were whistled for five misconducts on their way to a playoff-high 75 penalty minutes.

90 The return of Thornton brought the additional toughness and physicality to the Bruins lineup and he made that known on his opening shift, thumping Burrows with a big hit in the B's offensive zone.

91 Julien went on to publicly criticize the Canucks before Game 3 for their unsportsmanlike tactics, saying that type of behavior wouldn't be acceptable on his team. However, he forgot to tell his players! So when Lucic and Recchi engaged in those same taunting gestures during Game 3, Julien came away looking slightly hypocritical. He eventually filled the team in on what he said pregame and then reiterated that type of behavior is indeed unacceptable.

92 While Horton would not return to the series on the ice, his presence was felt symbolically in the Bruins dressing room. "Win it for Horty" became the Black & Gold's battle cry and the team decided that the Bruins jacket–which Horton had earned after his Game 7 winner against Tampa–remain in his stall until he was able to hand it out.

GAME 4 JUNE 8, 2011

VANCOUVER 0 BOSTON 4

Peverley took Horton's place on the B's first line and scored the B's first and fourth of the game[93] as Thomas stopped 38 for the shutout—his third of the playoffs. Postgame, Vancouver began to criticize Thomas' technique with Canucks defenseman Kevin Bieska describing Thomas as "leaky."

The series shifted to Vancouver tied 2-2 and the B's broke a club record with their 14th win of the postseason.[94]

---

93 Another instance of the Bruins depth up front coming through. By bumping Peverley from the third line to the first, and slotting Seguin in Peverley's old position, Julien was also able to leave the effective Recchi-Bergeron-Marchand line untouched.

94 The Bruins were treated to a surprise postgame guest, as Horton snuck into the locker room under the cover of the TD Garden security with about 5 minutes left in the game. Julien was filled in on Horton's presence and during his postgame comments said, "Now, I know you guys didn't want to give out the jacket unless Horty was here so..." And right on cue, a healthy-looking Horton appeared from behind the shower room curtain. To say the B's were happy to see their sidelined teammate would not do the scene inside the locker room justice. Dressed in a black suit and beaming with his trademark smile, Horton made some brief comments about how he was feeling better and proud of the team's effort that night. He then handed the jacket out to Peverley, the game's First Star.

TOP LEFT: Despite trailing the series two games to one, Bruins fans were confident their team would prevail. TOP RIGHT: Tim Thomas was perfect on the night with help from Zdeno Chara, *left*, frustrating Ryan Kesler, *center*, and his teammates. BOTTOM: Rich Peverley opened and closed the scoring on the night, *left*, which earned him the coveted postgame jacket presented in a surprise visit by Nathan Horton, *right*, and earned the Bruins a trip back to Vancouver with the series tied at two games apiece.

OPPOSITE TOP LEFT: Milan Lucic cleared pucks during warm-ups; they would be the only pucks that ended up in the Bruins net, as Tim Thomas notched his third shutout of the postseason.
OPPOSITE TOP RIGHT: Rich Peverley scored two of his four playoff goals in the series during Game 4. OPPOSITE BOTTOM: Despite the best efforts of Manny Malhotra, Thomas was a brick wall.
ABOVE: Brad Marchand sent Daniel Sedin flying in just one of the many confrontations between the two opponents that went Marchand's way.

GAME 5 JUNE 10, 2011

BOSTON 0 VANCOUVER 1

Luongo also got in a dig on Thomas after Lapierre scored the only goal of the game at 4:35 of the third period by saying he would have stopped the Vancouver goal because he plays in the crease and Timmy strays.

The next day Luongo, who took some heat for his comments, stood by his remarks and sounded hurt that Thomas hadn't been more complimentary of his work when he'd been "pumping his tires" all series.

Through the press, Thomas coolly responded, "I didn't realize it was my job to pump his tires."[95]

95 Thomas initially declined to comment on Luongo's remarks in this press conference. He was asked directly about what Luongo said and replied, "I did hear about what he said, but I don't really want to go into that." Later in the press conference however, a reporter rephrased the question slightly and asked, "I know you don't want to comment on what Roberto said, but he also said you didn't say anything nice about him. Did you want to comment on that?" That's when Thomas dropped the line of the playoffs.

TOP LEFT: Milan Lucic and Maxim Lapierre exchanged pleasantries during Game 5, but the Canuck would have the last word with the game's only goal. MIDDLE: After Vancouver goalie Roberto Luongo's, *bottom*, remark about the goal Tim Thomas allowed in the game, the Boston netminder, *top*, calmly responded with the quip of the postseason; No. 30 would not lose another game of the series, as the Bruins outscored Vancouver by a 9-2 margin in the final two contests. TOP RIGHT: *Left to right*: Lucic, David Krejci, Daniel Sedin, Rich Peverley, and Alex Burrows battled throughout the night. MIDDLE RIGHT: Tyler Seguin tried to break through the defensive duo of Sami Salo and Kevin Bieksa, while Luongo kept an eye on the action. BOTTOM RIGHT: Patrice Bergeron and Henrik Sedin faced off.

GAME 6 JUNE 13, 2011

VANCOUVER 2 BOSTON 5

Four B's (Marchand, Lucic, Ference, and Ryder) scored in a 4:14 span in the opening stanza to set a Stanley Cup record, while Recchi registered three assists. Luongo was chased after only 8:35 and he finished his three games at the TD Garden having allowed 15 goals. Coach Julien earned his 32nd postseason victory to set a team record for Boston and Marchand's marker represents a new rookie record for playoff goals.

"Not too many people counted on us being at this point right now," said Thomas, who won his last six playoff games at home and 10 of 11 overall.[96] "It's a great feeling. We battled hard tonight. We came to play and it's coming down to one game. This is what we dream of when we're little kids playing street hockey. We're going to go up there and we're going to go lay it on the line, like they are, and I think it's going to be an exciting game."

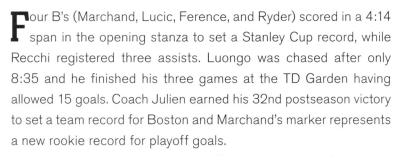

96 Thomas began a playoff pregame ritual of enjoying a toasted English muffin with peanut butter and strawberry jam approximately two hours before gametime in the Bruins players lounge. This ritual took place during the incredible playoff streak at home the Bruins were riding. He and the staff tried multiple times to replicate this tradition on the road by using the visiting hotel's ingredients, but were unable to produce the same results. The solution for Game 7? Pack all the items Thomas used from the player's lounge and bring them out to Vancouver. Sure enough, when he arrived to the rink for Game 7, he was treated to the familiar sight of his regular English muffins, his regular peanut butter, his regular strawberry jam, and even his regular toaster.

TOP LEFT: Coach Julien addressed the team prior to Game 6 while standing next to the chart that showed just two wins remained to their ultimate prize. BOTTOM LEFT: Tim Thomas' home pregame snack consisted of peanut butter and jam on a toasted English muffin; the ingredients—along with the TD Garden toaster—made the trip to Vancouver for Game 7. ABOVE: *Left to right*: Zdeno Chara, Michael Ryder, Andrew Ference, and Mark Recchi celebrated Ference's goal, which gave the team a 3-0 lead en route to a 5-2 win.

OPPOSITE: Tim Thomas saluted the fans following the Game 6 victory, hoping that the next time he greeted them would be from a duck boat.
ABOVE: Rich Peverley presented the victory jacket to Gregory Campbell, *top*, which gave the forward the honor of filling yet another piece on the Full 60+ chart, *bottom*.

Banner Captain

During the Bruins playoff run, the Fan Banner Captain was a former Bruin who put the Black & Gold's pregame ceremonies into gear by starting a giant B's flag on its journey around the loge section of the TD Garden. Meanwhile, in the balcony, the B's provided fans in the first row with numbered flags for every member of the Bruins, as well as the club's retired numbers.

During the 13 home playoff games, a very cool cross section of Bruins history materialized as the list of participating alumni included Rick Middleton, Ken Linseman, Lyndon Byers,

Reggie Lemelin, Terry O'Reilly, Stan Jonathan, Ray Bourque, John Bucyk, Ken Hodge, Derek Sanderson, Cam Neely, Bobby Orr, and Milt Schmidt.

Neely's turn—Game 3 of the Vancouver series—was significant because it marked the 25th anniversary of the team president's trade to Boston from Vancouver (as well as his birthday). The Bruins went on to score 8 goals that game, a coincidence that certainly brought a smile to No. 8's face.

Schmidt's turn before Game 6 was special, too, as the 93-year-old legend—the only man to captain, coach, and general manage the Bruins—brought the already excited crowd to another level of anticipation. But the most memorable moment belonged to none other than Orr. After he started the banner, Orr grabbed the Horton No. 18 flag and waved it in acknowledgement of the injured Bruins forward, further igniting the crowd. That helped set the table for Horton himself, who, just a few minutes later, was introduced on the Garden HDX at the first TV timeout.

And just like Game 3, the Bruins scored the same number of goals as their banner captain's jersey number, defeating the Canucks 4–0 on No. 4's night.

Fan Banner Captains

MONTREAL
Game 1: Rick Middleton
Game 2: Ken Linseman
Game 5: Lyndon Byers
Game 7: Reggie Lemelin

PHILADELPHIA
Game 3: Terry O'Reilly
Game 4: Stan Jonathan

TAMPA BAY
Game 1: Ray Bourque
Game 2: Johnny Bucyk
Game 5: Ken Hodge
Game 7: Derek Sanderson

VANCOUVER
Game 3: Cam Neely
Game 4: Bobby Orr
Came 6: Milt Schmidt

WALKING TOGETHER FOREVER

While the Bruins players settled in at their hotel[97] and began preparing for Game 7,[98] Bruins fans eagerly awaited the start of the biggest game in more than a generation. Even the relative calm of a morning walk in Vancouver wouldn't do much to give the fans in Black & Gold any sort of solace as they awaited the puck drop.

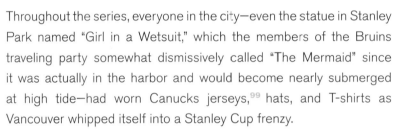

GAME 7 JUNE 15, 2011

BOSTON 4 VANCOUVER 0

Throughout the series, everyone in the city—even the statue in Stanley Park named "Girl in a Wetsuit," which the members of the Bruins traveling party somewhat dismissively called "The Mermaid" since it was actually in the harbor and would become nearly submerged at high tide—had worn Canucks jerseys,[99] hats, and T-shirts as Vancouver whipped itself into a Stanley Cup frenzy.

Every game was a public event, with crowds jamming into bars, restaurants, and the public spaces around Rogers Arena to watch every moment of every game and cheer their Canucks on to a victory that many saw as inevitable. It was a 15-day party, which most in Vancouver (and everyone everywhere else) seemed to think would continue throughout the summer.

Even the trip over to Rogers Arena for the clubs' final confrontation contributed to the Bruins siege mentality as the team, who had been cloistered for many days during the series in their hotel on the edge of downtown Vancouver, watched out their windows as nearly every person they saw made sure they knew exactly what the blue and green-clad Canucks fans thought of the Black & Gold.

In many ways, it felt like Boston had been invited to a coronation, with the Canucks being the royalty and the Bruins—providing just enough entertainment—playing the jester's role. However, prior to Game 7 the Bruins players sounded very grounded in the knowledge that no matter the majesty of the moment, the club that kept its collective head out of the clouds might be the team to inspire the magical moments in the future.

"Right now, that's what it is—it's a dream," Kelly said. "We need to go out and have our best effort."

But CBC's cameras captured Horton, who had traveled with the B's although he was unable to play, giving a little extra effort of

97 Bergeron approached Recchi at the team meal the night before Game 7 on June 14. Knowing what was at stake and knowing that this wasn't Recchi's first Stanley Cup rodeo, he asked the veteran how he was approaching tomorrow's game. Recchi calmly said, "Just play our game. Going to go out there and have fun like I always do. Not do anything different."

98 Following the meal, Bergeron threw on his iPod and went for a stroll on the famed Vancouver Harborwalk. Listening to a heavy dose of hip-hop, his focus was as sharp as it's ever been. He began visualizing himself and his line performing well in Game 7—visualizing faceoffs, forechecking, skating, scoring. He returned to his hotel room and did more of the same, even watching YouTube highlights of some of his best goals, putting himself in a positive frame of mind. Before he went to sleep, Bergeron recalled a poem he wrote for a school assignment when he was 12 years old. The assignment was to write a poem about something that meant a lot to him. His choice? Hockey, of course. The poem—inscribed in pencil—now sits in a frame in his parents' house in Quebec City. Written in French and titled "Le Hockey," Bergeron begins, "My dream started from my first stride. From that moment I was dreaming of the day that I would get that trophy. It was my destiny." He goes on to write, "I dream of the day that I will lift up the crowds all across the country proving them that this is my sport" and concludes with "I'm on a breakaway toward a goal that I've always dreamed of getting. And I will get it!"

99 Director of Hockey Administration Ryan Nadeau went for an early morning jog around Stanley Park the day of Game 7. At approximately 5:30 a.m. he ran by the "Girl in a Wetsuit" and was surprised to see her now sporting a Bruins T-shirt. Someone—presumably a B's fan—had ventured out into the rocky surf, scaled the statue and placed the shirt over the Canucks jersey. Just moments later, a jogger clad in full Canucks sweats headed toward him from the opposite direction. As the jogger approached closer, Nadeau noticed it wasn't just any Canucks fan, it was the team's Head Coach Alain Vigneault. Safe to speculate that the Canucks bench boss could not have been pleased to see the famous Stanley Park landmark donning the enemy's colors the morning of the biggest home game in his franchise's history.

OPPOSITE: Zdeno Chara prepared to hand the Stanley Cup to Mark Recchi to start the traditional Cup skate; Recchi played his final game in Game 7 in Vancouver on June 15, 2011, ending his Hall of Fame career with his third championship ring.

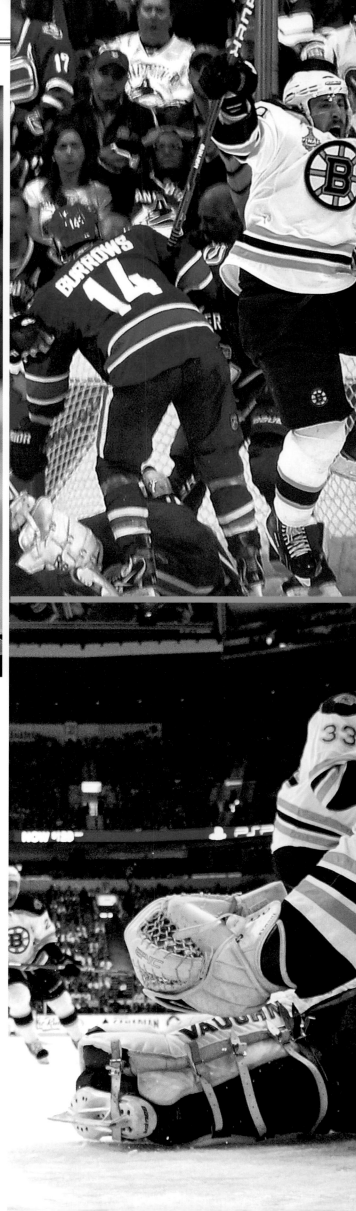

his own. In a move that would make any Standells fan happy, the injured right wing poured some melted Garden ice, real dirty water, onto the rink at Rogers Arena two hours before puck drop.[100]

"I was just trying to get some Garden ice here and make it our ice," Horton said afterward. "I was trying to be sneaky about it."

With gametime less than one hour away, positivity, focus, and determination were reverberating through the Bruins locker room.[101] A memorable pregame speech by Assistant Coach Geoff Ward provided some extra motivation[102] and there was a lot of chatter amongst the players—more than usual—as the B's taped their sticks, laced their skates, and wrapped up their final pregame preparations.[103]

Upstairs in the suites, Jeremy Jacobs, Charlie Jacobs, and nearly their entire family were on hand, eager to finally deliver on their

ABOVE: Tim Thomas stood in contemplation during the national anthems prior to Game 7. TOP RIGHT: Brad Marchand, *left*, celebrated giving the Bruins a 2–0 lead as Zdeno Chara, *center*, and Patrice Bergeron, *right*, joined him. BOTTOM RIGHT: Thomas set a club record with his fourth shutout of the playoffs in the 4–0 Game 7 victory.

100 The "Water Bottle" idea was hatched by Assistant Coach Geoff Ward and his friend Dale Adams after Game 6. Knowing the team's struggles in Vancouver were drastically different from

their dominance at home, Ward cryptically asked the equipment staff to bottle up shavings from center ice at the TD Garden and bring them to Vancouver for Game 7. On the afternoon of Game 7, he explained to the equipment staff what the purpose was. Hockey tape was placed along the top of the Gatorade bottle and in black marker, one side was labeled "Our Ice," the other "Garden Ice." Ward instructed the trainers to find Horton when the winger arrived and tell him that "this is ice from home. Use it to make their ice, our ice." Horton excitedly agreed, did what was asked, and was caught on camera in the process. Word of what Horton had done quickly trickled back to the locker room and the Bruins loved it. While the whole scenario appears as a small, inconsequential action in the grand scheme of the Final, its symbolism was important to the Bruins in their preparation. It gave the players a positive motivational tool that helped them mentally get ready for Game 7.

101 "It's out of our hands now boys, but I trust each and every one of them out there to get the job done," extra defenseman Shane Hnidy remarked to the other players not in the Game 7 lineup. "This is like a movie where I know there's a good ending," he said. "I just want to fast-forward to the end."

102 Written by Ward earlier in the afternoon, this "speech" was originally intended to be a letter to his children, with the purpose of passing on lessons learned in confronting a monumental day such as this one. When he arrived to the rink later in the afternoon, he showed the letter to Julien, who thought it would be great to read aloud to the team before the game. During the speech, Ward encouraged the players to "get in touch with that inner voice that we respect and listen to and comforts us during crazy times–whether it be a father, mother, wife, or old coach." "What would that voice say to you today?" he asked. "Keep your head in the things you can control, your effort and intensity, your jobs in the flow of the game," he continued. He then encouraged the Bruins to be positive, aggressive, and play with no fear, as "fortune favors the bold." "Hard work and clear focus beat talent," Ward said. He finished by declaring, "Do not be afraid to succeed! Win together today and we walk together forever."

103 Bergeron approached Marchand and asked the rookie how he was feeling. "Good man, I'm ready," said Marchand. Bergeron could tell by Marchand's demeanor that he was telling the truth. The pair then pulled their other linemate, nearly 20 years their senior, aside. "We need to be the line tonight that gets everyone going," they vowed. "We need to step up. It starts with us."

LEFT: Defensemen Zdeno Chara and Dennis Seidenberg cleared the front of the crease, allowing Tim Thomas to see everything coming his way in the Game 7 victory. TOP RIGHT: Vancouver's Kevin Bieksa looked on as Johnny Boychuk unleashed a shot from the point. MIDDLE RIGHT: Andrew Ference and Jeff Tambellini battled along the boards. BOTTOM RIGHT: Mark Recchi got by two Canucks in front of the Vancouver net, but Roberto Luongo made the save.

promise to bring the Cup back to Boston for the first time under their stewardship. Even higher in the arena, Neely, Chiarelli, and Assistant GMs Don Sweeney and Jim Benning were stationed in the press box,[104] knowing that they were only 60 minutes away from achieving the one goal that had proved to be so elusive in their respective playing careers.

Once the game started, the B's best effort, perhaps buoyed by Horton's water from Boston, overwhelmed the Canucks. Early in the first, it was the Bruins fourth line of Shawn Thornton, Gregory Campbell, and Daniel Paille that got things going by repeatedly hemming the Canucks in their own end with a physical, aggressive forecheck.[105] They set the tone early and the rest of the B's seemed to feed off of their energy.

Bergeron opened the scoring at 14:37 of the first thanks to a pretty play by Marchand, who would add his own goal at 12:13 of the second off helpers from Seidenberg and Recchi.[106] Bergeron netted his second goal, a shorthanded tally, with assists going to Seidenberg and Campbell[107] and with a 3–0 lead by the end of the second period, staffers in

ABOVE TOP: Patrice Bergeron, *left*, put the B's up by a 3-0 margin, scoring his second of the game with a shorthanded tally. BOTTOM RIGHT: Brad Marchand had an unsettling effect on Vancouver's Daniel Sedin all throughout the series.

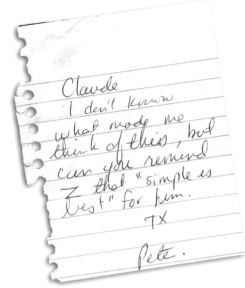

Claude
I don't know
what made me
think of this, but
can you remind
Z that "simple is
best" for him.
TX

Pete.

104 Cell phone service was poor in the upper regions of Rogers Arena. During warm-ups, Chiarelli had attempted to send a BBM (BlackBerry Message) to Julien. Because of the weak signal, the message never was delivered, forcing Chiarelli to come up with an alternative way to get his note to the head coach. The B's GM scribbled his note on a piece of notebook paper and had it delivered downstairs to the locker room.

105 "Those were the three guys that got us going," said Lucic of the B's energy line. "I think the role that Campbell played this whole year gets overlooked a lot. I think without him, we don't win. He was big in so many ways."

106 Recchi nearly had a goal-of-the-postseason candidate after dangling through the Vancouver defense with a burst of speed not seen from the 43-year-old in years. His attempt was thwarted by Luongo however. "If I was younger, I'd finish that boys!" declared Recchi to his teammates in the locker room during the second intermission. When asked about this impressive display months later, Recchi laughed and remarked "I don't know where that came from."

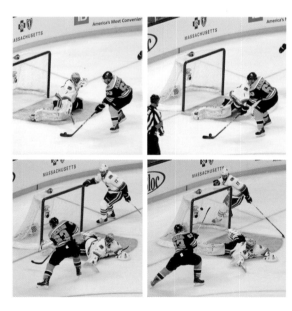

107 Despite facing teams that finished first (Vancouver), sixth (Tampa) and seventh (Montreal) during the regular season in power play percentage, the Bruins penalty killers were stellar with a man down in the playoffs. In the Final, they actually scored more goals shorthanded (3) than the Canucks scored on the power play (2). Although he is quick to hand all the credit over to his killers, Assistant Coach Doug Houda deserves praise also, as he headed up the P.K. units and was responsible for coordinating the video breakdown and scouting sessions.

Black & Gold, as well as the players' families, allowed themselves to believe that nearly four decades of frustration were coming to an end.

However, the Bruins players continued to keep playing—hard.

"I know that before we went out for the third period, everybody in there was telling each other that there was no way in the world that we could even let up for a second and that we had to play a full 60 minutes," said Julien.[108] "And that's been our team for these playoffs, a 60-minute effort because they've heard me say it all year."

Thomas finished the game with 37 saves and when Marchand scored his second into an empty net with 2:44 remaining,[109] it was fans in Boston who were peacefully streaming toward the TD Garden to celebrate the city's latest crown, even as many Vancouverite's emotions spilled over into the streets.

Inside Rogers Arena, however, the B's, who outscored the Canucks 23–8 in the Final, became the first team in NHL history to win three Game 7's on their way to capturing the Stanley Cup. Boston also set an NHL record for fewest goals against in a seven-game series as Thomas joined Bobby Orr as the only Bruins ever to win the Conn Smythe Trophy as playoff MVP. [110]

ABOVE: Brad Marchand, *left*, and Patrice Bergeron, *right*, each scored twice in the 4–0 Cup clinching victory. TOP RIGHT: Craig Campbell, *left*, and Phil Pritchard, *right*, carry the Stanley Cup onto the ice for NHL Commissioner Gary Bettman's, *center*, presentation. MIDDLE RIGHT: Goaltenders Roberto Luongo and Tim Thomas shared a moment during the postgame handshake line. BOTTOM RIGHT: An injured Nathan Horton, *right*, joined Andrew Ference, *left*, and all of his teammates on the ice for the postgame celebration.

108 Julien ended his second intermission talk to the players by saying, "This has to be our best 20 minutes of the f#*^% year."

109 The intense focus of the Bruins in this game—and their adherence to the "full 60 minute" mantra—is no more evident than after Marchand scored the empty-netter. Now carrying an insurmountable 4–0 lead with less than three minutes left, the Bruins bench jumped up and celebrated briefly, only to immediately sit back down, put on their game faces and focus on their next shift. When watching the video after the fact, the players laughed at how serious the team was after that goal, given the game's circumstances.

110 A little known fact about the Conn Smythe Trophy? It's sharp! Thomas actually got scratched multiple times on his chest by the trophy's maple leaf when he was posing for pictures.

With a soundtrack that included Dropkick Murphys' "Shipping Up to Boston" and, of course, "Dirty Water," the Bruins exchanged the Cup with one another after Chara nearly toppled in his sincere excitement.

Afterward, Chara said that his favorite moment (besides raising the Cup, of course) was when, as he skated toward Lord Stanley's silver bowl, he looked back at his teammates lined up along the blueline, and pointed at them. The rest of the Bruins returned his salute. Chara said it was the best exchange a leader could have.

Coach Julien said he was content to enjoy the view. "The best way is always to stand back and watch everybody else enjoy it and enjoy it through their eyes."

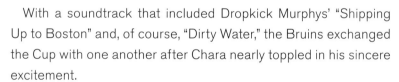

ABOVE TOP: Captain Zdeno Chara started the locker room celebration by spraying his teammates with champagne. ABOVE BOTTOM: *Left to right*: Michael Ryder, Chris Kelly, and Tyler Seguin kept the Cup in close contact. OPPOSITE TOP: Milan Lucic prepared to take a drink from the Cup amid the chaotic dressing room scene. BOTTOM LEFT: Steven Kampfer poured a beer into the Cup from one of the commemorative aluminum bottles. BOTTOM RIGHT: *Left to right*: Shane Hnidy, Zdeno Chara, and Rich Peverley shared a celebratory moment.

Boston fans throughout the world were doing the same thing.

Inside the locker room, family members joined the team on the ice after everyone on the B's travel party had hoisted the Cup and when the ebullient Bruins flowed back into Rogers Arena's visitors' locker room, the bubbly flowed freely.[111]

There were two orders of business left, however: the final pie piece needed to be added to the Full 60+ puzzle and the jacket needed to be handed out one final time. The locker room was cleared of everyone except the players, coaches, and the team support staff. Julien gave his closing remarks[112] and Campbell passed out the jacket to Recchi,[113] who just months earlier had stated that if the Bruins won the Cup, this would be his final season.[114]

Back in Boston, preparations were being made for a celebration unlike anyone from New England had seen since 1972 and the city began a party that wouldn't end until the last duck boat returned to the TD Garden parking lot several days later.

"They made it tough, we just kept pushing hard, we wanted to battle," said Marchand. "We wanted to prove we were the better team...and we did."

ABOVE: Zdeno Chara, *top left*, Charlie Jacobs, *top right*, Patrice Bergeron, Colby Cohen and Daniel Paille, *bottom left*, and Michael Ryder with Milan Lucic and a napping Nathan Horton, *bottom right*, all spent part of the ride home with the plane's most important passenger. TOP RIGHT: Chara deplaned at Logan Airport with the Cup held aloft. It was the end of a nine-and-a-half-month journey that saw the team fly 65,316 miles starting with their season-opening trip to Europe. BOTTOM RIGHT: Chara shared the Cup with club staffers who were waiting to greet the victors when they returned to the TD Garden.

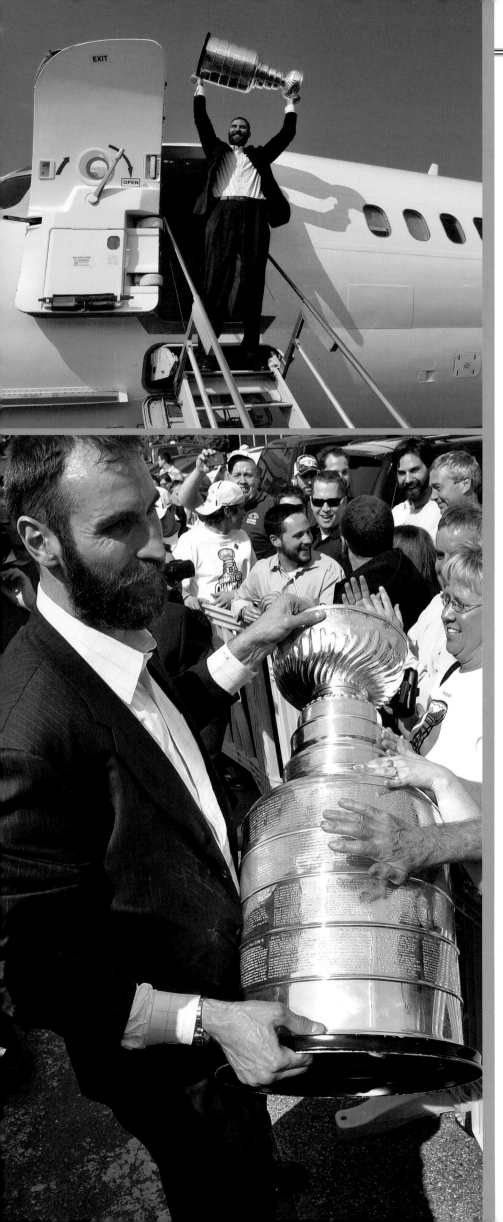

111 "It's one thing to win the Stanley Cup and having my childhood dream come true, but it means even more because we did it with our friends," Bergeron told Ference as the two embraced amidst the champagne showers. "We wanted to do it for each other," he said. "And that is why we won."

112 "I'm so proud of you guys," beamed Julien. "I wanted it more for you guys than you can even imagine. To see you guys rewarded, that just made my whole career."

113 Campbell quieted the room down and said, "To be honest, anyone in the whole room could get this jacket right now. That's why we won. But I know that if any one of us could have 1/8th of this guy's career we'd be pretty happy." He then called Recchi up and handed over the jacket.

114 Recchi was the last to speak in front of the team. "This is it for me," he said in reference to his retirement. "This year has meant the world to me, regardless of what happened tonight. This is the best group I ever had in 22 years. I've had an amazing time."

My Dream

By Zdeno Chara

I remember before I signed with Boston Bruins in 2006 I told my wife, Tatiana, "I really want to win the Cup. I really believe we can do it with Boston."

If you are reading this, you can probably recall the image of me skating toward the Stanley Cup and getting it from Commissioner Gary Bettman. I almost couldn't believe that I was skating toward my dream, but you might have missed the moment just prior to my picking up the Cup. As I skated to the table, I thought about the ultimate goal I set five years ago for the Boston Bruins organization, for the fans, for all the kids playing sports, simply for all of the people in Boston. I also thought about all the things that we have been through together as a team: the injuries, the ups and downs, and the tough losses. But most of all, when I turned around and pointed at my teammates, I was thinking of them. I wanted to show them that I was going to get the Cup and that none of this would have happened without all of them. The whole team.

I was really emotional. I screamed. I was bouncing the Cup in my arms so hard that I knocked my hat off my head. I was nearly falling down with excitement as I skated back to my teammates. As a leader and captain, you want to let those people around you know how important their contributions are. No matter the role, ice time, age—we are all as one. You also hope that your teammates understand that when you are tough on them, demanding, that you are only doing it for the good of the team.

When the final buzzer sounded, I knew that we had just accomplished the ultimate goal, a Stanley Cup championship. And when I pointed at them and they pointed right back—I have to tell you as a father, husband, friend, captain, I couldn't have had a better exchange with the guys than that.

Getting the Cup and bringing it back to them as champions, that was, for me, a dream come true.

CHAPTER NINE
SHORT, SWEET SUMMER

On December 16, 1773 Bostonians let the world know exactly what they thought of British oppression (and the Crown's latest tax) and, in a colorful act of protest, threw three shiploads of tea into Boston Harbor. Ever since the "Boston Tea Party"—a benchmark on America's road to revolution—people around the globe have understood that New Englanders know how to throw down.

Add a 39-year wait to Boston's penchant for party planning and you had a victory celebration for the ages.

It took six champagne-soaked hours, but when the B's finally arrived home from Vancouver after Game 7,[115] the plans for Boston's latest rolling rally were almost complete.[116] The club and the city announced that the traveling show would begin at the TD Garden on Saturday, June 18, at 1ˉ a.m., move through the city via Causeway, Staniford, Cambridge, Tremont, and Boylston streets and end at Copley Square.[117]

By the end of that gorgeous late spring day, more than 1.5 million people would jam the streets in Boston in peaceful celebration of their beloved Bruins.[118]

"I only have a few things to say," Thomas said to the crowd gathered in front of the Garden before the Black & Gold boarded 18 duck boats. "I want to say, you guys wanted it, we got it and we want to share it with you today."

In addition to the full team, staff, and executives, the Bruins mascot Blades, anthem singer Rene Rancourt, the Bruins official organist Ron Poster, the B's Ice Girls, and members of the Bruins and the TD Garden staff all traveled by duck boat as well.

The entire team clearly enjoyed the outpouring of emotion and stoked the city's enthusiasm by acknowledging the fan's high expectations throughout the Cup run.

"You guys have been saying a chant during the playoffs about 'We want the Cup,'" said Bergeron. "Well, you know what, we got the Cup! We got the Cup! We got the Cup!"

The Bergy-led chant began in the TD Garden lot and reverberated on all the way through the Back Bay to the John

115 The Bruins were treated to a hero's welcome upon touching down at Logan. Boston Fire Department boats sprayed their hoses in the air, ambulances and police cars sounded their sirens, and airport employees gathered near the plane applauding the champions, thrilled to be the first Bostonians to see the Cup back on New England soil.

116 Once they landed, Neely went directly to City Hall to meet with the Mayor's office to hammer out the celebration plans with the city's Parade Planning Committee. His suit stained in champagne and cigar smoke—and visibly tired from the previous night's (and morning's) festivities—he apologized for his appearance and asked for the committee's understanding. Given the special circumstances, the Mayor accepted his apology without hesitation.

117 Friday the 17th and Saturday the 18th were the two parade dates being considered. The wrench in the date selection? Saturday night's Katy Perry concert. Friday was logistically the easier option, as the parade could take place during the day with no impact on the load-in for her staging trucks, which was originally scheduled for Friday night. However, the Bruins, the TD Garden, and the Mayor's office deemed Saturday to be the better day from the public's standpoint. Garden staff worked it out with Perry's tour organizers to reschedule the load-in for Saturday afternoon after the rolling rally ended. Good thing this worked out, because had the rally been set for Friday, it would have rained on the Bruins parade—literally.

118 Boston Police confirmed it was the largest parade in the history of the city, besting the '02, '04, and '05 Patriots, '04 and '07 Red Sox, and '08 Celtics.

OPPOSITE: Confetti rained down on Duck Boat Longfellow Bridget during the championship parade.

Hancock Tower, over the Harvard Bridge and the Charles River, and back to the West End as the duck boats made their tour and looped home through Cambridge. Along the way, Bruins fans from all over the hockey world screamed, smiled, chanted, or simply said, "Thank you."[119]

Chara, who hadn't stopped smiling since he got the Cup from NHL Commissioner Gary Bettman on Wednesday, slowed the parade several times in order to let fans touch hockey's Holy Grail. Everywhere along the route the roads were lined with fans in Black & Gold stacked hundreds deep. Side streets were also impassible, but only a few arrests were reported as the Boston Police called the B's rolling rally the most successful of the Hubs' many championship celebrations over the past decade.

---

119 As Recchi's boat rolled by, fans hollered, "One more year! One more year!"

TOP LEFT: Mark Recchi saluted the crowd as he rode off into the sunset of his career, having retired following the Game 7 win. CENTER: The duck boats made their way down Boylston Street as the parade neared its conclusion. TOP RIGHT: The boats began their journey from the TD Garden front lot. MIDDLE RIGHT: The crowd that gathered to cheer the team on June 18 was estimated to be the largest ever for a Boston championship parade. BOTTOM RIGHT: Owner Jeremy Jacobs hoisted the Cup with Tim Thomas from the lead boat.

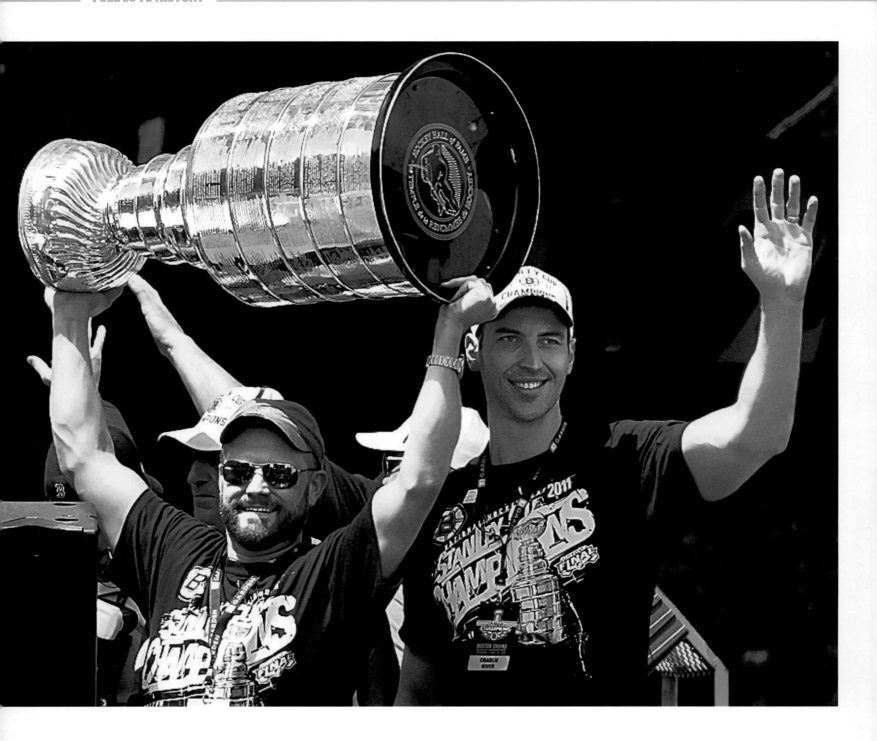

"It was more overwhelming than I expected," admitted Thornton, an Oshawa, Ontario native who is now a year-long resident of Charlestown. "It was an unbelievable turnout. I didn't know that many people lived in Boston, let alone be on the streets today.

"It was an awesome, awesome experience."

That was really no great shock. Chiarelli was praising B's supporters even before he saw the hundreds of thousands of people who had come to Boston to greet the Black & Gold.

"You guys are the best fans in the world," he said. "You make the players better, you make the management better, you make the coaches better."

There's no doubt that the fans' demand for a winner had altered the way that the Bruins played hockey, but the Bruins faithful had evolved, too. The Hub of Hockey had re-made itself into the ultimate NHL city, which now held hockey's ultimate prize for the summer.

"It's going to be a short summer, but it'll be a good one in Boston. That's for sure," Thornton said.[120]

120 Days in between the Stanley Cup Champs' last game of the 2010–11 season and start of training camp? 92. Days in between the Montreal Canadiens' last game of the 2010–11 season and start of training camp? 142. Days in between the last game of the 2010–11 season for teams who didn't make the playoffs and the start of training camp? 166.

JOHNNY BOYCHUK 55

TICKETS & DEPARTURES PRUDE CEN

CLOCKWISE FROM TOP LEFT: Tim Thomas and Zdeno Chara, Johnny Boychuk and Dennis Seidenberg, Charlie Jacobs and Cam Neely, Peter Chiarelli, and Shawn Thornton all acknowledged with heartfelt thanks the outstanding response of the crowd.

Before the team split for the summer, the Bruins enjoyed a well-documented night out at Foxwoods,[121] followed up by hopping on the duck boats one more time and taking them inside Fenway Park to throw out the first pitch before the Sox-Brewers game on Sunday, June 19.[122]

Once the team festivities ended and the players headed home, the Bruins had the Cup for 100 days and each member of the traveling party and executive staff had "The Jug" for most of a day as the chalice traversed the world from Wilmington, Massachusetts to Niagara Falls to Toronto to Europe[123] and back to Vancouver.

Ference and Thornton's days with the Cup back in Boston stretched the celebration until it was nearly time for the Black & Gold to take to the Garden ice for the 2011–12 season.

"We have a neighborhood that we live in and you add all the things together we have a lot of really close friends here in Boston," he said. "On top of that, it means a lot to this city, you know? If this was the type of city that wasn't so passionate about their hockey then I probably would have taken it home [to Canada]."

ABOVE: Zdeno Chara, silhouetted against a rain of confetti. RIGHT: David Krejci's gesture left no doubt as to how the team finished their season.

121 Much was made of the Bruins astronomical bar tab the night of their Shrine Nightclub gathering at the MGM Grand at Foxwoods. The inside story? The hotel rooms (the whole fourth floor) were provided free of charge by Foxwoods. Additionally, the private security, bus transportation from the TD Garden to the casino and back, bowling, dinner, and the drinks at the nightclub (including the massive $100,000 bottle of Ace of Spades Midas champagne, which was to be signed by the team and auctioned off for charity) were all complimentary. The Bruins did not have to pay for anything that night, they were only responsible for tipping the bartenders and servers. While no one on the team denies the legitimacy of the $156,679.74 receipt or its contents, the tab they actually paid is nowhere near that amount.

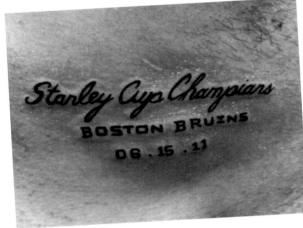

122 After the first pitch, the team headed straight to the Garden for their "Breakup Day" meetings with Chiarelli and Julien and to clean out their lockers. One of the players also arranged for a tattoo artist to set up a studio in the Bruins locker room hallway for anyone interested in getting a permanent reminder of their Stanley Cup accomplishment. Marchand was interested; he selected *Stanley Cup Champions* in script above Boston Bruins in block letters with the date the team won the Cup at the bottom and had the artist go to work. Marchand proudly went to show off his new ink to his teammates, but after he peeled off the bandage Campbell laughed and pointed out a fairly glaring error. "*Champions* is spelled wrong," Campbell said. Unfazed at first, Marchand thought he was joking but when he checked the mirror the misspelling was confirmed the tattoo read *Champians*. Marchand raced back to the artist to see about having the "a" transformed to an "o." Luckily, the tattoo was still fresh, and he now—and forever—bears the mark of a *Champion*.

123 The European stops on the journey included Kladno, Czech Republic (Kaberle); Sternberk, Czech Republic (Krejci); Bratislava and Trencin, Slovakia (Chara); Savonlinna, Finland (Rask); and Helsinki, Finland (Scout Jukka Holtari).

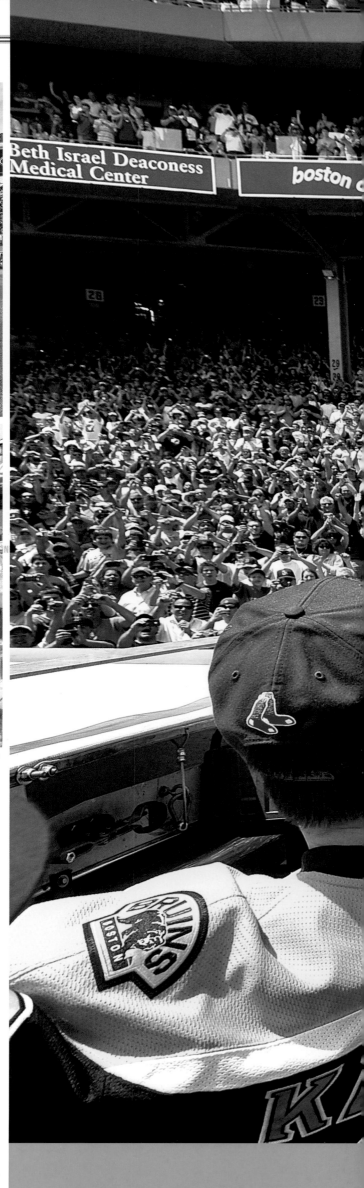

"It's a great place," continued Ference. "They've been great to me and it's like home to us, just as much as anywhere else."

"The people have been unbelievable to me ever since I got here," said Thornton, who asked the powers-that-be to give him a little extra time with the Stanley Cup in order to give back to Boston.[124] "The organization, the Hall of Fame, and the NHL were very gracious about giving me a day here on top of the one I had in my hometown.

"We've taken it to a couple of local establishments and all the people seem to be having a good time with the trophy, so I think everyone is getting a kick out of it.

"You see all the smiles on everyone's faces and that's pretty cool."

124 The players who received multiple days with the Cup were Chara (Bratislava and Trencin, Slovakia), Recchi (Kamloops, British Columbia and Boston, Massachusetts), Bergeron (Quebec City, Quebec x 2), Thornton (Toronto, Ontario and Boston, Massachusetts) and Tim Thomas (Davison, Michigan and Burlington, Vermont).

The Bruins celebration continued at Fenway Park on June 19 as Zdeno Chara led the team onto the field, *top left*, to throw out the first pitches; the champions greeted the Sox in the clubhouse, where, *bottom left, left to right*, Andrew Ference, David Ortiz, Zdeno Chara, and Kevin Youkilis posed for a photo. ABOVE: Patrice Bergeron hoisted the Cup accompanied by Tomas Kaberle and Andrew Ference while the boats lapped the field.

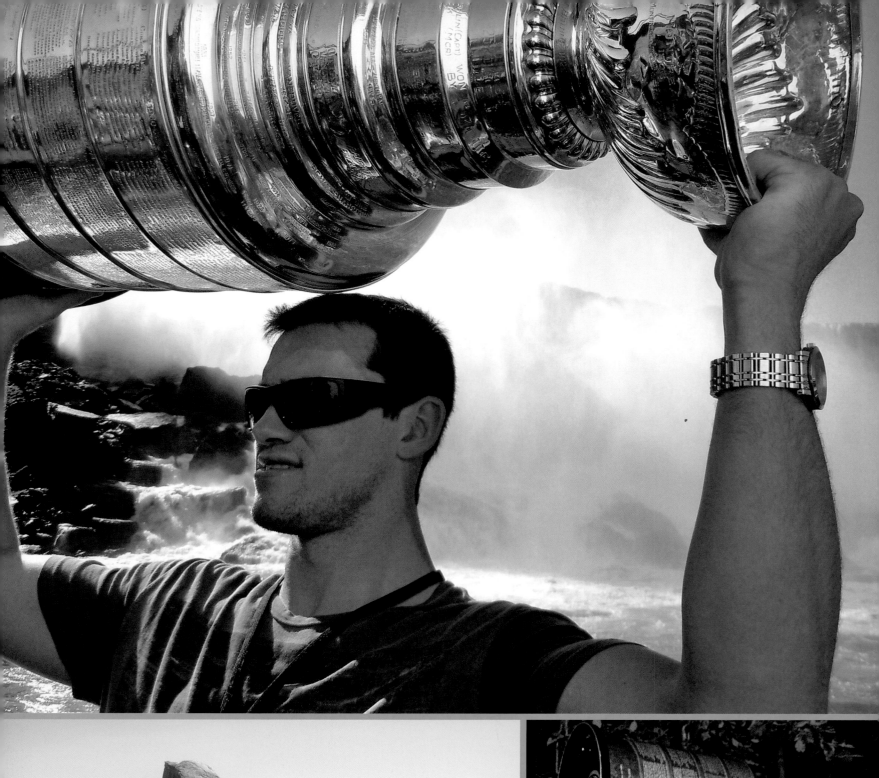

The Cup's summer player tour included stops in, *clockwise from top left*, Niagara Falls with Daniel Paille; Trencin, Czech Republic with Zdeno Chara; Michigan with Tim and Melissa Thomas; Quebec City's famed Chateau Frontenac with Patrice Bergeron and family; a Finnish hot tub with Tuukka Rask; and Yosemite National Park with Jeremy and Peggy Jacobs.

CHAPTER TEN

TURNING THE PAGE

The waning moments of the 2011–12 preseason were a whirlwind for the Stanley Cup champions. Early October saw the club travel to Great Diamond Island, Maine for team bonding centered around turning the page on the 2010–11 season. During those private sessions Head Coach Julien consistently reminded his players, "Last year we learned how good we *can* be. This year we need to learn how good we *have* to be."[125]

However, when the Bruins returned to Boston, the team enjoyed two more significant Stanley Cup events.

On October 4 nearly all of the 2011 Stanley Cup championship team (including the now retired Hnidy and Recchi, as well as Ryder, the Dallas Stars' newest forward) enjoyed dinner at the Boston Harbor Hotel. There, the Jacobs family rewarded the players, coaches, and staff with an incredible token of their esteem.[126]

The crest of the fabulous Boston Bruins 2011 Stanley Cup ring featured diamond set images of the iconic spoked-B logo and the Stanley Cup against a background of white gold.[127] Six larger diamonds on the crest of the ring represented the B's six Cups and the diamond-covered top of each piece was framed on the left side by "STANLEY CUP" and on the right side by "CHAMPIONS."[128] On the opposite shoulder, the player name, secondary logo, and player sweater number surrounded by six stones honoring the B's as being one of the Original Six hockey franchises.[129]

Even the band of the ring was intricate as the playoff slogan that decorated the locker room during the championship run—"FULL 60+ TO HISTORY"—was engraved on the inside of the band,[130] as were the opponent logos and series scores of the playoffs.[131]

"It's a really special piece," said Campbell of his first look at the ring.

"The ring is something that's always been a symbol of a championship team and to actually receive the ring and put it on, it's a unique feeling. It's just the same as lifting the Cup on the ice after the game."

125 Julien also had a new motivational quote put on display in the Bruins locker room, which hangs above the interior locker room doors: "Demolish the bridges behind you…Then there is no choice but to build again." This was meant to reinforce the theme that the Bruins need to start over in 2011–12 and begin the process of building toward another Stanley Cup championship from scratch.

126 Charlie Jacobs, Neely, Chiarelli, SVP of Sales and Marketing Amy Latimer, and Matt Chmura headed up the Bruins internal ring design committee. The design process began during the Bruins Development Camp in early July and continued through the end of August. During this time, the committee viewed approximately 30 championship rings from different professional leagues, including those of the Patriots, Celtics, and Red Sox. They ended up seeing 20 different variations of the Bruins ring before settling on the final design. The week of August 26th when the design was finalized, Neely had a sample flown to him on Martha's Vineyard during his vacation. The club's president wanted to see the final version in person (not just in a photograph) before giving his final approval.

127 Nine out of the last 10 Stanley Cup championship rings incorporated both the Stanley Cup and the team logo on the crest. The Bruins ring committee liked that tradition and wanted to find a design that paid proper tribute to the Cup and made the spoked-B stand out. They toyed with the idea of incorporating black and canary-colored diamonds, but ultimately felt those didn't look as impressive as the all-white.

128 One player ring contains a total of 302 diamonds.

129 The secondary logo was chosen because it features the word "Bruins." Up until that logo was added, "Bruins" had not appeared on the ring.

130 Other than the player rings, only one other ring contains the "Full 60+ to History" engraving on the inside of the band: Graphic Designer Jason Petrie's. The committee felt it appropriate to recognize Petrie for his contributions to the playoff slogan.

131 The order of the opponents on the band engraving goes clockwise from Montreal, Philadelphia, Tampa Bay to Vancouver. This was intentionally done to mirror the order they appeared on the "Full 60+ to History" stopwatch poster.

OPPOSITE: The 2011 Stanley Cup Champion Boston Bruins took their final team photo with the Cup and newly minted banner.

At Rowes Wharf everyone's reaction was similar to Campbell as the collective gasp from the players, management and their wives in attendance was audible, but followed by a stunned silence.

"I got a BBM from Looch as soon as we opened those boxes saying, 'You know what? It was all worth it,'" Campbell recalled. "The organization did a great job at really personalizing those rings and making it special to our team."

The Bruins organization had gone to great lengths to ensure that their world-beating championship squad would have a world-class memento and Principal Charlie Jacobs explained the gratitude he felt toward his club earlier in the day.

"Personally, from my experience here in Boston, this season made it all worth it," he said. "I mean, regarding the hardships of the league and those years that we weren't necessarily as successful as we aimed to be [and our goal is to] continue these winning ways that we've experienced this past year."

At the ring ceremony itself, his father Jeremy reiterated those sentiments.

"I can't tell you how much this meant to me to watch you all celebrate with your families, friends, and communities," said Jacobs. "This truly has been a special few months. The spoked-B means dedication, grit, determination, and team above all else. These rings are lasting symbols of what it means to be a Bruin—a lifelong reminder of this incredible special time."

"It's hard to believe that on Thursday, we begin it all over again."

ABOVE: The players were greeted by a huge Stanley Cup banner upon their arrival at the Rowes Wharf red carpet; the same banner would be passed around the crowd at the home opener two days later. MIDDLE TOP: Milan Lucic's smile matched the shine of his ring. TOP RIGHT: Tim Thomas shared his delight with his table mates. MIDDLE RIGHT: Jeremy Jacobs asked Neely and the rest of the Bruins organization to raise their glasses during his congratulatory toast on October 4, 2011, just prior to unveiling the Stanley Cup rings for the first time. BOTTOM RIGHT: Closeups of the amazing rings, *left to right*, of Tim Thomas, Zdeno Chara, Patrice Bergeron, and Mark Recchi.

Lucic, for one, said he was very much looking forward to that night.

"It's something that nobody is ever going to be able to take away from us."

But going into October 6, the night the B's raised their sixth banner to the TD Garden rafters, Julien continued to dare his group not to be satisfied with their singular accomplishment.

"Let's not pretend here that there's no emotion in raising the banner and reliving what happened, but I think this is what will be the final step of what we need to do as a team," Julien said. "As far as I'm concerned, our fans and the city of Boston can celebrate this as long as they want because they deserve it and they are entitled to it, but we as a team have a job to do and that's to start all over again."

"That's good, because none of the 17,565 fans in the building were in any hurry to move forward as quickly as their hockey team, as a fabulous celebration was in store for the Hub of Hockey."[132]

A fan fest, which featured a big screen replay of Game 7 in Vancouver, jumpstarted the evening, but a parade put the party in motion. Police, fire, and military personnel from all over New England and a youth hockey team led a Stanley

---

132 The organization began their planning for the opening night festivities back in mid-July, with the intention of creating a grand celebration that was true to the Bruins organization and true to the team's history. One of the challenges of the ceremony was coming up with a creative way to unveil the actual banner, which the B's marketing, game presentation, and operations groups led by Chris DiPierro, Fred Bowen, and Joao Rebelo accomplished by utilizing the kabuki-style screen.

OPPOSITE: With the Kabuki screen dropped, the TD Garden fans got their first glimpse of the banner. TOP RIGHT: Mike Bolt and Phil Pritchard carried the Cup under a canopy of hockey sticks held by fire, police, and military personnel. BOTTOM RIGHT: Bruins Owner Jeremy Jacobs accepted the Cup, as he had the honor of bringing it into the building for he night's festivities.

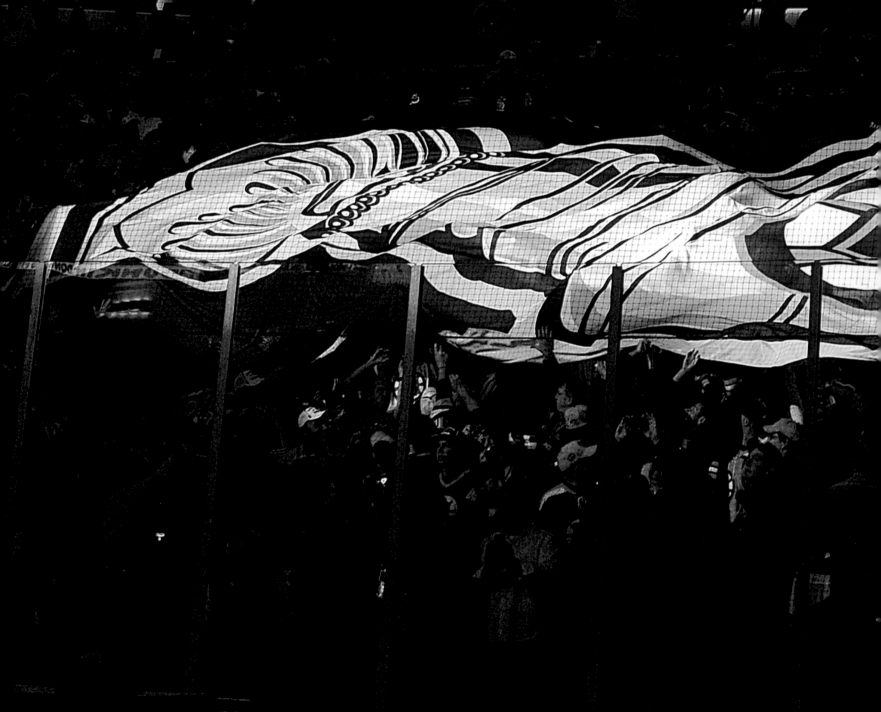

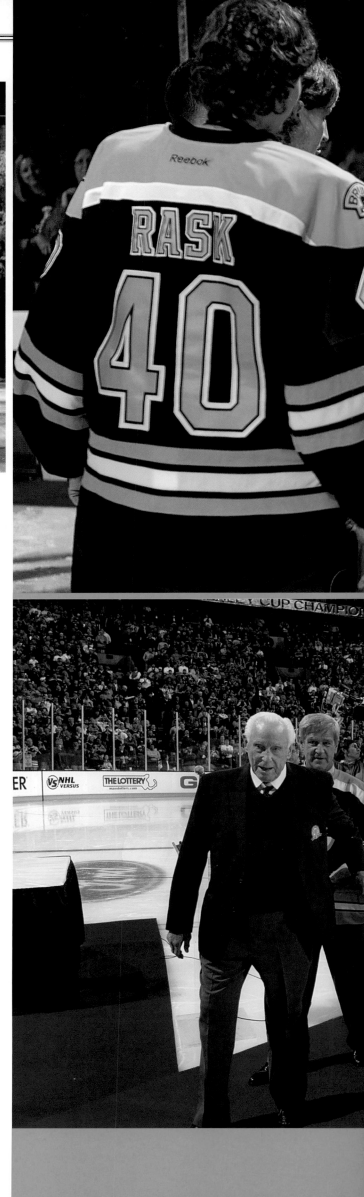

Cup parade down Canal and Causeway streets.[133] Then the Cup was escorted through the uniformed formation and "White Glove Stick Salute" all the way into the building, where it was welcomed by nearly the entire Jacobs family and Bruins alumni.

With energy reminiscent of the previous spring's playoffs, a special Stanley Cup Fan Banner was passed around the loge after warm-ups concluded.[134] The TD Garden lights were dimmed as the arena's video boards, Garden HDX, and a huge kabuki-style screen draped from the scoreboard at center ice recounted the B's history-making season. Finally, the screen dramatically dropped to unveil the Bruins sixth Stanley Cup banner. Led by Chara, the players then skated on to the ice and passed the Cup in front of their delighted home fans.[135] Recchi and Hnidy were in full gear as well, and each Bruin had a chance to hoist the Cup on Garden ice.

Neely stepped to the podium, where he said to the fans (and no doubt to the players seated behind him), "What do you say we do it again, guys!"

Recchi and Hnidy had returned to the ice in uniform to skate with the Cup. When Ference—now wearing Recchi's alternate captain's

---

133 More than 500 military, fire, and police personnel participated in the parade, representing all six New England states.

134 Neely recommended using a banner with the Stanley Cup on it so that Bruins fans could participate in the celebration by symbolically passing the Cup to one another.

135 It was Chara's idea to pass the Cup to all of his teammates and have everyone hoist it in front of the Bruins fans. Due to time constraints, the ceremony's program allotted time for Chara to skate a lap around the rink with the trophy (the rest of the players would follow behind him) and then he would bring it to the table at center ice. However, just as he had done in May when he organized the team photo with the Prince of Wales Trophy and again on June 15 when he pointed back at the team before lifting the Cup for the first time in Vancouver, the Bruins captain wanted to share this special moment with all of his teammates.

TOP LEFT: Zdeno Chara led his teammates onto the TD Garden ice to skate with the Stanley Cup for the first time. ABOVE TOP: The great Bobby Orr greeted the Bruins as he entered the ice to participate in the pregame celebrations. ABOVE BOTTOM: *Left to right*: Bruins Cup-winning alumni Milt Schmidt, Bobby Orr, John Bucyk, Ken Hodge, Todd Bailey (representing his father Ace), Derek Sanderson, John McKenzie, and Don Marcotte carried one side of the banner, while Zdeno Chara led his teammates on the other side.

"A"—gave out the jacket to Recchi, he said, "He taught us what it meant to be champions."[136] Dressed in his full game gear, Recchi put the jacket on over his pads and wore it one final time.[137]

Finally, after a 39-year wait, the moment had come and Causeway Street would raise another Black & Gold championship flag.[138]

Representatives of the 1972 Bruins Stanley Cup championship squad, including Orr, Bucyk, and Milt Schmidt, helped Bergeron, Chara, Recchi, and Thomas transport the banner from center ice, through the B's brass, and coaching staff to cables waiting to lift it high.[139]

The 2011 banner finished its ascent to the Garden rafters and settled into its new neighborhood, closing the curtain on the Boston Bruins sixth Stanley Cup season and opening the team's pursuit of number seven.

"That was a special moment," Thomas said.

"While it was happening I was picturing myself coming back and visiting for a game 30 years from now and looking at that banner and saying, 'We helped raise that banner.'"

And when Thomas does come back for that visit 30 years from now, hopefully there will be a number of other, newer banners right alongside the one he helped raise in 2011.

ABOVE: Captain Zdeno Chara, *left*, and President Cam Neely, *right*, addressed the fans during the ceremony.
RIGHT: The sixth Stanley Cup banner in club history was raised to the rafters as the team looked on.

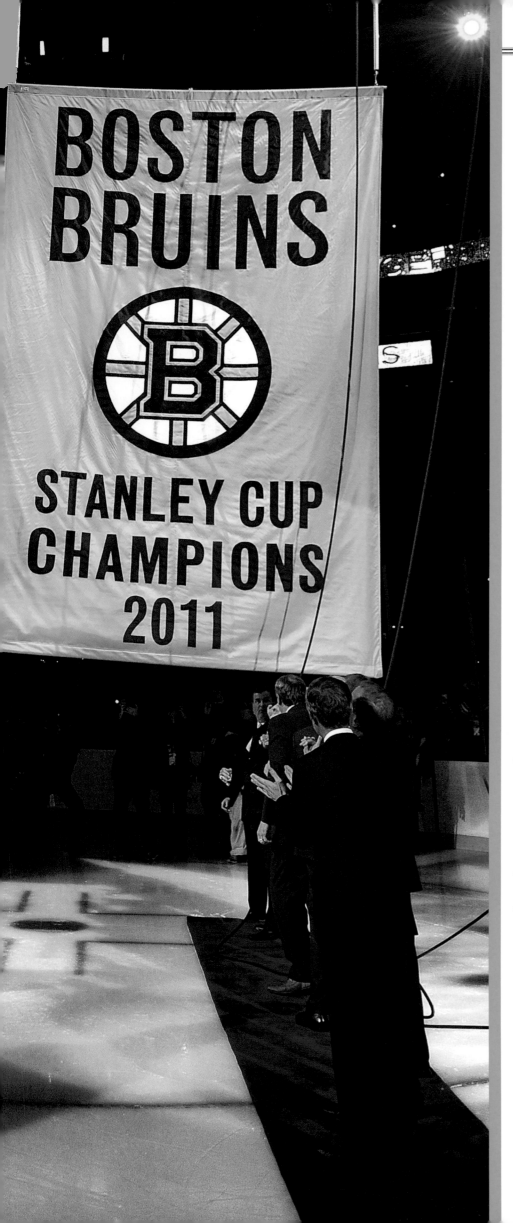

136 Ference had rehearsed this speech earlier in the day at home in his shower. And not just the words, he practiced the intonation, tempo, and emphasis as well. "That wasn't a situation I wanted to go into unprepared!" Ference exclaimed when asked if he had memorized the speech beforehand. The "situation" he is obviously referring to is speaking in front of the 17,565 people in the arena and hundreds of thousands at home watching on television.

137 The jacket presentation to Recchi was a surprise to everyone on the team besides Ference. When he received the jacket, Recchi was overwhelmed with emotion. The host of the ceremony Andy Brickley asked Recchi if he wanted to say a few words to the crowd, but he respectfully declined. Later that night, Recchi said the reason he declined was because he wouldn't have been able to make it through his speech without breaking down.

138 The instrumental track that was played during the banner raise was called "Titans Spirit" and composed by Trevor Rabin.

139 If you review the video of the banner raising closely, you can see Chara reach out and touch the banner one final time as it starts making its way up to the rafters. When asked about this after, he was surprised anyone noticed. "It was almost like saying goodbye to a friend," the captain explained, who likened it to a farewell handshake or fist bump with someone you enjoyed spending time with but now had to leave. And with that small, subtle gesture, the Bruins captain closed the book on the 2011 championship season.

AFTERWORD
MARK RECCHI

I have been fortunate. I won the World Juniors, the Turner Cup, and the Stanley Cup all within a span of four years and all by the age of 23. Fifteen years later, I won it all a second time. But winning the Stanley Cup last year as a Boston Bruin was extra special.

I came to the Bruins from Tampa Bay at the trade deadline in 2009. I'd heard Boston mentioned as a possible destination, and while there were other teams in the mix, I was hoping Boston was where I would go because I'd seen what they were doing, I knew they had a chance to win, and I wanted to be part of it.

We lost a tough series to Carolina in the Eastern Conference semifinals that season but that was nothing compared to losing to Philadelphia in the semis in 2010. I didn't want my career to end like that, but then again I was 42 years old. I thought we had the makings of a special team in Boston and I thought I could help. That's what I told Peter Chiarelli and Claude Julien after the season, and fortunately they wanted me back. I was excited to take one more crack at it.

Going into training camp, I had no doubts that we were one of the top teams. Management had made the right offseason moves, and the coaches had a powerful message. Claude made sure we talked about having ended the previous season with such a tough loss to the Flyers. We cleared the air and agreed that we had to learn from it and get better because of it to become that team that can get to the next level. The team trip to Northern Ireland and Prague also proved to be a tremendous stepping stone for us. I've been around long enough to have pretty much seen it all, and I could see that this team was completely committed.

We made it back to the playoffs last season and faced Montreal in the first round. We knew it was going to be a tough series—there was just so much animosity between two teams—but we did not expect to lose the first two games on our home ice. The thing was, I had been through the exact same scenario with Carolina in 2006: losing the first two at home to the Canadiens. I was able to share with our guys in our locker room my experience of having come back to win. We returned the favor and took the next two games in Montreal before the series went to Game 7 in Boston. That game could've gone either way, but I think we wanted it more.

We exorcised a lot of demons in our rematch with Philly in the second round, sweeping the Flyers in four straight. We were clearly the better team, but what I think that series really showed was how we were able to take what happened the year before, put it in the past, and build on it.

The interesting thing about playing Tampa Bay in the conference finals was that there wasn't anybody to hate. It builds energy when you're angry and you don't like the other team, but we just didn't have that hate for Tampa Bay, so we had to find other ways to beat them. We split the first six games, and then in Game 7 we played our best game of the playoffs. It was playoff hockey at its best; neither team had a single penalty, which had not happened in 20 years. We won 1-0. It was just an unbelievable feeling to be headed back to the Finals.

Before the start of the Vancouver series the media reported that I'd said I would sail off into the sunset if the Bruins won it all. What I said was there was no way I'd be able to train because I was planning to party all summer after winning the Cup. I said it jokingly, but I knew all along it would be my last season.

The formal announcement came after we'd won the Cup and Ron MacLean asked me, "Is that it?" I said it was, absolutely, as there was no better way to end a career than playing with the Boston Bruins, an Original Six team, with that group of guys. It meant as much to me to watch my teammates hoist the Cup as it meant for me to hold it aloft one last time.

This fall, it was a weird feeling not to go back to training camp. I'm helping coach my son's squirt hockey team, which has been keeping me busy, and I've started working out again. I took three months off. I didn't do anything. That was the first time in 25 years, so it felt good but eventually I had to get back into shape—not because I'm expecting my phone to ring, but if the Bruins get in a pinch, they know where to find me.

ACKNOWLEDGMENTS

BOSTON BRUINS

PROJECT DIRECTOR & EDITOR
JEN COMPTON

WRITERS
JOHN BISHOP, ERIC TOSI

ASSISTANT EDITORS
MATT CHMURA, CHRIS DIPIERRO

PHOTOGRAPHY DIRECTOR
HEIDI HOLLAND

CREATIVE DIRECTOR AND COVER DESIGN
JASON PETRIE

SKYBOX PRESS

EDITOR
SCOTT GUMMER

PUBLISHER
PETER GOTFREDSON

CREATIVE DIRECTOR
NATE BEALE

PROJECT MANAGER
VICTORIA SCAVO

The Boston Bruins wish to thank the many members of the organization who contributed to the creation of this book in a variety of ways; without their diligence and effort, *Full 60+ to History* would not have been possible. In the front office, we are grateful for the support of the Marketing, Communications, Interactive, and Finance departments, as well as the Boston Bruins Proshop. We are especially appreciative of the management and players who took the time to author their own pieces: Jeremy Jacobs, Cam Neely, Peter Chiarelli, Claude Julien, Zdeno Chara, Patrice Bergeron, Andrew Ference, Mark Recchi, Tim Thomas, and Shawn Thornton, as well as the other players and staff who made themselves available for interviews and helped us recap our unforgettable season.

Additional thanks to Tiffani Fleming, Jill Marr, Ken Coburn and the team at Global Interprint, Dennis Alpert, and Dean McCausland.

PHOTOGRAPHY BY:

NHLI VIA GETTY IMAGES: **Abel, Graig**, Pg. 172; **Aller, Justin K.**, Pgs. 25, 47, 102-104; **Audette, Scott**, Pgs. 103-104; **Babineau, Brian**, Pgs. 6-7, 12, 14, 19, 21, 24, 30, 34-35, 40-41, 45, 52, 68, 72-73, 78-81, 84-85, 93-95, 110-111, 116-117, 120-121, 123, 126-128, 130-131, 134. 136-137, 139-140, 142, 148-149, 152-153, 156-157, 174, 179-183, 186-187, 190; **Babineau, Steve**, Pgs. 2-3, 23, 28, 42-43, 47, 51, 54-55, 57, 59, 64, 66, 70-71, 73, 95, 98-99, 101, 106-107, 124-125, 138-139, 146-147, 157, 173, 179, 182-186; **Chytilova, Jana**, Pgs. 56-57; **Devlin, Andy**, Pgs. 56, 58; **Lacasse, Francois**, Pgs. 74-75, 78-79, 83; **MacCallum, Phillip**, Pgs. 74-75, 78, 82-83; **Redkoles, Len**, Pgs. 60-61, 88-90; **Ringuette, Andre**, Pgs. 24-25; **Sandford, David**, Pgs. 16, 22, 48, 118, 128, 144-147, 149, 152, 156; **Shamus, Gregory**, Pgs. 44-45, 47; **Vinnick, Jeff**, Pgs. 10-11, 56, 118-121, 142-143, 145, 149-151; **Wippert, Bill**, Pg. 48.

GETTY IMAGES: **Abelimages**, Pg. 23; **Bennett, Bruce**, Pgs. 23, 42, 62-63, 88-89, 92, 94-95, 100-102, 105, 116-117, 130-131, 149, 156-157, Inside Back Flap; **Bereswill, Paul**, Pgs. 90-91; **Cox, Kevin C.**, Pgs. 49-50; **Elsa**, Cover, Pgs. 18, 20, 23, 40, 46, 59, 72-73, 80-81, 86, 92-93, 106, 122, 134-135, 143, 186; **How, Harry**, Pgs. 4-5, 49, 116, 122-123, 129, 131-133, 145, 147, 153, 157; **Laham, Nick**, Pg. 36; **Lam, Rich**, Pgs. 114-115, 130-131; **Pasatieri, Christopher**, Pg. 45; **Rogash, Jim**, Pgs. 84-85, 101, 110-111; **Schechter, Eliot J.**, Pgs. 59, 102-105, 108-109; **Stobe, Mike**, Pgs. 97-98.

BOSTON BRUINS: **Babineau, Brian**, Pgs. 10, 20, 25, 28, 31-33, 37, 64-65, 67- 70, 87, 96,110, 123, 128, 154-155, 159, 161, 168-169, 172-173, 175-177, Back Cover; **Babineau, Jamie**, Pgs. 158, 160, 165, 178, 188-189; **Babineau, Steve**, Pgs. 8-10, 13, 27, 62, 112, 123, 128, 149, 160-161, 176-177; **Bergeron, Patrice**, Pg. 141; **Collins, Kerry**, Pg. 59; **DelNegro, Don**, Pg. 41; **Gotlib, Jonathan**, Pgs. 76-77, 79, 155, 171; **Ivins, Michael**, Pgs. 161-163, 166; **Lanzel, Sheryl**, Pgs. 59, 96, 166-167; **Owens, Angela**, Pgs. 164-165; **Petrie, Jason**, Pgs. 41, 96; **Tosi, Eric**, Pgs. 111, 113, 134, 143, 147, 167, 170-171

ADDITIONAL: **Elevate Communications**, Pg. 167; **Falkenstein, Chris**, Pg. 170; **Gomez, Christian**, Pg. 171; **Hohenadel, Karin**, Pg. 170; **Levin, Eric / elevin studios**, Pg. 26; **Mullen Advertising**, Pg. 192; **Nelligan, Pamela J. / Courtesy High 5 Adventure Learning**, Pg. 29; **Pickett, John**, Inside Back Cover; **West, Matt**, Pgs. 106-107

3920 Conde Street, San Diego, CA 92110
www.skyboxpress.com

An imprint of Luxury Custom Publishing